School Leadership—
Balancing Power
with Caring

School Leadership—
Balancing Power
with Caring

KATHLEEN SERNAK

FOREWORD BY NEL NODDINGS

Teachers College, Columbia University
New York and London

Published by Teachers College Press, 1234 Amsterdam Avenue, New York, NY 10027

Library of Congress Cataloging-in-Publication Data
Sernak, Kathleen.
    School leadership—balancing power with caring / Kathleen Sernak ; foreword by Nel Noddings.
        p.   cm.
    Includes bibliographical references and index.
    ISBN 0-8077-3762-3 (hardcover : alk. paper). — ISBN 0-8077-3761-5 (pbk. : alk. paper)
    1. Educational leadership—United States—Case studies.   2. School management and organization—United States—Decision making—Case studies.   3. School-based management—United States—Case studies.
    4. Caring.   I. Title.
    LB2805.S54   1998   98-27054
    371.2—DC21

ISBN 0-8077-3761-5 (paper)
ISBN 0-8077-3762-3 (cloth)

Printed on acid-free paper

Manufactured in the United States of America

05   04   03   02   01   00   99   98   8   7   6   5   4   3   2   1

To my children, Kim and Kent Johnson, the essence of my life, and to my mother, Eleanor Sernak, who has always believed in me.

Contents

Foreword

Kathleen Sernak has written a powerful and somewhat disheartening book. It is powerful because it depicts in vivid language the struggles of real people in a difficult, but increasingly familiar, situation. It is disheartening because the people described here want to care and just cannot bring it off. Indeed, for me (as a "care theorist"), it is doubly disheartening. First, any reader will feel sorry for the principal, teachers, university people, and community members who "care" and yet cannot connect with one another; and, of course, one aches for the students who are the ultimate victims of so many miscarried efforts to care. Second, Sernak's moving story points up dramatically a major misunderstanding about the nature of care, and this is troubling for care theorists. There is evidence, throughout the book, that people define caring as a virtue, as an attribute belonging to individuals. This is a mistake that often leads to hurt and confusion.

Perhaps the most important contribution that care theory has made to the practice of care is to emphasize caring as a relation. In ordinary usage, "caring" can certainly refer to a virtue. We often say, for example: "He is a caring person." "She cares deeply for children." "Nurses are more caring than doctors." In all of these cases, we construe caring as a virtue. However, a more important sense of caring points to a relation. A caring relation is one in which the carer attends and responds appropriately to the needs of the cared-for, and the cared-for somehow acknowledges that the care has been received. From this perspective, it is futile to insist that one cares, if the recipient of care denies that he or she has been cared for.

In literature, this is the heart of tragedy—characters acting bravely (and stubbornly) on their own sense of care or justice and failing entirely to establish relations of care and trust. In Sernak's account, readers will meet a courageous principal, Mattie, who is deeply caring in the virtue sense but unable to create caring relations with her professional staff. Acting from firm religious convictions, Mattie responds to individuals with touching care when they share personal problems with her. But she does not do what a caring leader must do; she does not establish the conditions under which caring relations can flourish.

Sernak introduces the notion of caring power to describe what is needed in such situations. It is not enough for a leader to care for individuals in a personally responsive way, although she must, of course, do this. One cannot just "manage" caring; one must model it. But, as a leader, a principal must also use his or her power to build structures and institute procedures that will support caring throughout the web of care. Leaders who use caring power must ask: Will this strategy, structural change, or policy help to establish, maintain, or enhance caring relations? If not, how can we modify it so that care is preserved? Instead, the leaders in this account (and, sadly, in so many others) argue that they are enacting unpopular measures because they "care."

One of the most heartbreaking stories told here is that of the failed ninth-grade experiment. In this episode, an ambitious teacher has planned a promising program for a cadre of ninth-grade students. The plan fits much of what we believe about enlightened practice in curriculum, pedagogy, and school structuring. It has the tentative backing of both university partners and the site-based steering committee. But, ostensibly because other teachers on the proposed team are unenthusiastic, Mattie refuses to give her support. A wonderful opportunity to provide better education is lost, and the fragile web of care is further weakened.

Sernak has made a major contribution to our understanding of care as a virtue by describing both its uses and abuses. In her discussion of caring power, she has underscored the reason for studying care as a relational attribute, not a virtue. More than personal vision and assertiveness, educational leaders need qualities that will enable them to model caring relations and to establish the conditions under which caring relations will thrive.

Nel Noddings

Acknowledgments

As with all else in my life, the completion of this book is a result of the assistance and friendship of many people. Professionally, several colleagues have mentored me in this and other projects. I thank specifically, David Labaree and Anna Neumann, who encouraged me to publish this book. Jim Greenan read several versions of the manuscript, each time providing extensive and pertinent suggestions. Mark Seals, a graduate student who believes that effective teaching and caring are inseparable, continuously challenged my thinking and understanding concerning caring and power, and continues to do so. Jill May was eager to discuss various ideas about caring and culture, enough so that she sat in on a graduate class I taught. She also made me laugh and take time to see the humor in tense situations.

On another level, Brian Ellerbeck of Teachers College Press, provided the sensitivity and understanding I needed at fallow times in my writing and in stressful periods in my personal life. I also thank Lori Tate for her sharp eye in editing.

Friends were most important to me as I worked on the manuscript. Eileen Steele listened, offered support when asked, and continuously reinforced me as an academic, as a writer, and as a person. Jay Hayes invited me to write at his desk, where I could look out on lovely expanses of grass, flowers, trees, and fields, and where I could divert myself with kittens cavorting on the lawn. He was also there for me when I cried.

Most of all, I thank my mom and my children for caring enough to always stand by me and to celebrate our lives together.

Introduction

Peace does not mean an end to tension, the good tensions, or of struggle. . . . It means being centered.

—May Sarton, *The House by the Sea*, 1981

This is a story about caring, which, as it developed, was not the one I anticipated telling. My intention was to study educational leadership and organizational structure in relationship to an ethic of caring. I planned to study a principal whom I admired as a nurturing woman and educator, and her faculty and staff as they attempted to transform a school with a high student dropout rate and a reputation for crime, violence, and drug dealing, into an institution that provided students, teachers, and staff with education, support, and mutuality to "fully be" (Noddings, 1989).

Many of the faculty and staff had been at that building for over 20 years, experiencing the "rise and fall" of what once was the premier school of the district. Many were bitter, approaching burnout, scarred from the past, and clinging to a last fragment of hope that their teaching would make a difference. The principal, new to the school, brought with her a reputation for caring, which fanned the barely glowing embers of enthusiasm among the faculty. Finally, site-based management and shared decision-making, although not initiated by staff members, held for some of them the potential for cooperation and collaboration between administrators and staff. For those reasons, I chose to study the creation of an ethic of caring in that particular school.

I anticipated the principal's interacting with individual staff members and students, as I had seen her before: sympathetic/empathetic, understanding, and supportive. Because previous faculty members had characterized her as often tough but fair—someone they could always go to with any problem, personal or professional—I envisioned the new staff reacting to her with admiration and respect, responsive to her caring for them. I expected them, in turn, to model her example, thereby nurturing relationships between and among themselves. With site-based management and shared decision-making would come opportunities for administration and staff to work together on common goals, to collaborate on the decisions, and to take mutual responsibility for implementing and assessing processes and outcomes. Organizational change would enable staff and administrators, especially the principal, to develop

1

trusting relationships and to experience mutual dependence, both necessary to caring.

The anticipated actions and reactions did occur, but not always in the ways I thought they would. The principal spent much time with teachers who sought her solace and understanding, or whom she gently encouraged to share their burdens with her. Her personal relationships flourished in the first months of her position as chief administrator, allowing individual teachers to feel as though they, at long last, had a leader who cared for and about them. Staff opened themselves to the possibility that they could trust her, that they could begin to make changes in the school.

The faculty's enthusiasm grew, and with that came a myriad of ideas for change from various groups within the school. But with those notions came responsibility for ensuring that changes benefited the whole school and that they fit within its mission and aims. Individuals and groups of teachers felt rebuffed and controlled when the principal did not support their particular ideas. The principal, subsequently, became a target of contempt. Her actions, intended as caring, were interpreted, or misinterpreted, as using power to benefit her own position rather than the school's reputation.

Site-based management and shared decision-making reinforced a feeling of control, rather than caring, among faculty. The school community had a history of extreme distrust between staff and administration. It balked at the mandate from the district office to implement site-based management since there was no model for either the administrators or the staff to follow. The directive split the staff into union faculty who supported the initiative, and nonunion faculty who felt it was a union ploy to control them. Consequently, site-based management and shared decision-making became for many teachers simply another vehicle through which the multitiered school and district and/ or union leadership could exercise power over any number of groups and individuals within the school. Ultimately, the teachers associated the principal with site-based management which, in turn, they linked to increased power over, not caring about, them.

I was not so naive as to think there would be no problems or that all faculty members would feel cared for, or cared for to the same degree. But I did think they would perceive acts proffered as caring as just that. I was mistaken. Early into my study, power not only became a major issue, but was linked to acts that I perceived as caring. The latter caused me to reconsider my perception of what it meant to care. My story, then, became a story of caring *and* power, for I began to see the impact of power on caring and the *integration* of power and caring, a caring *with* power.

My story is on two levels. The primary narrative is of the struggles of a principal, teachers, and staff to create a caring school community within a traditional, bureaucratic hierarchy based on authority and control. Tensions created by underlying power structures become evident, and the notion that caring involves power unfolds. Establishing a school that is a caring place requires caring for more than discrete individuals: Such a school necessitates nurturing the individuals as a whole community and as groups within the whole. My observations and conversations caused me to question whether there may be a need to use one's power in order to establish a foundation from which caring can grow in an institution like school, that is, in an organization that is hierarchical and that values competition, individuality, and universality.

Underlying that story is the emergent awareness of my need to understand the connection between power and caring, that is, my need as a woman, mother, friend, and educator to know how I care and how that need drove my research. The total narrative embodies not only an intellectual and academic description and interpretation of the data, but also a reflection of the conflicts and tensions I experience as a "caring person." In the process of analyzing the data, I became aware of my having to face the fears I have of personally being too controlling and dominating under the *guise of caring for others*. I thought about my administrative experience when, at times, I believed I needed to use power in order to effect a result that ultimately was caring. I remembered times when I took control or used my authority to bring about what I thought was in the best interests of an individual or a group, and I was wrong. And I recalled instances where I believed I acted in a caring manner, but the recipients saw my efforts as controlling or self-serving. Consequently, I began to read and listen to the interviews differently, for the struggles the teachers and principal experienced became my own. My experiences caused me to consider the possibility that caring may be inseparable from power. If so, how do they work together to nurture a caring place?

No longer were there saints and sinners, those who cared and those who wielded power. I recognized people who lived the question: What is the relationship between caring and power? My research, therefore, extends beyond solely a study of caring to posit the idea of an integral relationship between caring and power. Furthermore, I suggest that when the goal is to establish an institution, a school, for example, as a caring place, the use of power may be necessary in order to create a climate of care benefiting many persons, in addition to the caring between two individuals.

Although much has been written about the particular concepts of caring and power, few theorists have written about the integration and linkage between caring and power. Those who have written about such a connection, have studied a teacher and her students. Virtually nothing has been written about the concept of caring *and* power from the perspective of leadership and school organization.

As a participant observer in this school, I desired to study the attempts that the principal and her faculty made to effect changes that would make their school more caring. Because the history of the school and the people were so important to the story, I drew on feminist standpoint theory based on the politics of identity and location (Harding, 1986, 1987, 1991; Krieger, 1991; Luke & Gore, 1992; Weiler, 1988) for data analysis, as well as interpretive research assumptions and methods (Bogden & Biklen, 1982; Hammersley & Atkinson, 1983). Following are the types of data collected:

1. Field notes. Each day I wrote descriptions of what I observed in the school in various places, such as the cafeteria, classrooms, main office, counselors' waiting room, and teachers' lounge; and of activities I attended, such as student convocations, athletic events, and prom preparations. I also recorded my understandings of informal conversations with faculty members, administrators, counselors, security guards, and students. I followed the descriptions with reflections relating to theoretical inconsistencies with my understandings of power and caring and what I observed.

2. Documents. I collected all the minutes from the following: Site-Based Management Steering Committee, Professional Development School (PDS); School–Business Collaborative; and faculty meetings. Those minutes provided a historical perspective of the relationships of those groups to the faculty and administration. I also collected student newspapers from 1966–1972 and 1991–1993; they provided a history of the school.

3. Audiotapes. I taped PDS meetings; ninth-grade team meetings; and faculty meetings. These provided a perspective on current interrelationships between groups within and outside the school, and between faculty and administrators, and of the then current concerns of the faculty.

4. Interviews. During the first semester my interviews focused on the principal. In addition to semistructured, formal interviews, we had many informal conversations in the halls or in her office. I aimed to understand how she perceived herself as caring, what she did as acts of caring, how she perceived faculty members in their caring of her and of each other, what she understood as her power, and how she understood power over her. Second semester interviews focused on teachers. Thirty-three faculty members participated in interviews. The Site-Based Management Steering Committee chairperson was interviewed three times, and three members of the ninth-grade team were interviewed three times; the remainder of the teachers participated in one interview each. The focus of the interviews was on the participants' perception of caring and power as exhibited by the principal and by other faculty members.

In this book, I examine caring from three perspectives, introduced by a discussion of tenets that Noddings (1984) identifies as necessary aspects of an ethic of caring. I begin with a critique of an ethic of caring from the perspectives of caring within leadership, caring as a female ethic, caring for a collective, and caring as a cultural concept. The following chapters consider descriptions and examinations of the principal's, the collective faculty's, and specific faculty groups' perspectives on caring, and how those understandings relate to perceptions of power. I conclude the book with the suggestion that there is an integral connection between caring and power; the view that power is necessary to caring, but not the reverse; and the idea that there are indications for "caring power" as the basis for school reform.

My critique of an ethic of caring suggests that it is really a politics of caring. It calls into question the accepted tenets of, as well as assumptions associated with, caring. The subjects discussed are (1) caring as a "female ethic" (Grimshaw, 1986); (2) the downside of caring as connection (Baker Miller, 1976; Fisher & Tronto, 1990), community (Fox-Genovese, 1991; Tronto, 1987, 1993), and reciprocity (Fisher & Tronto, 1990; Grimshaw, 1986); and (3) caring as cultural understanding, which is rarely considered or acknowledged in organizational structure (Dillard, 1994; Eugene, 1989; Lykes, 1989; Taylor-Guthrie, 1994).

Before addressing the intents and actions of the principal and the faculty in relation to caring and power, I present the histories of Division High School (DHS) and Newtown,[1] the town in which the school is located. The historical background is integral to understanding the perceptions of caring and power held by many of the faculty participants. An examination of the principal's role in developing a climate conducive to caring follows. I view caring in the context of the principal's leadership as an African American woman with the task of creating an atmosphere of nurturance for the faculty and staff as a whole. Using Noddings's characteristics of caring—collaborative, situational, reciprocal, and committed (Gilligan, 1982; Noddings, 1984)—I discuss the principal as she cares for individuals and as she attempts to care for the collective, that is, for the faculty and staff as a whole. Following are descriptions of ways in which faculty and staff perceive the intents and actions of the principal, one caring, for them, the ones cared-for (Noddings, 1984). I further describe ways in which they nurture themselves as a collective and as smaller, interdependent groups within the whole. Through those discussions, I begin to explore the notion of a connection between caring and power.

Finally, I examine the interrelationship between caring and power. I do that within the framework of a discussion of the potential impacts of caring power on leadership and organization of schools, particularly as educators weigh the options of various cultural and educational needs involved in school reform initiatives. We need to challenge schools to be caring places, but within the context of power relationships and with the intent of transforming those into relationships of caring power.

CHAPTER 1

Genesis of a Story

Women seek a reconstruction of relationships for which we have neither words nor models: a reconstruction which can give each person the fullness of their being. . . . We seek a new concept of relationships between persons, groups, life systems, a relationship which is not competitive or hierarchical but mutually enhancing.
— Rosemary Radford Ruether, *New Woman, New Earth*, 1975

This story begins and ends with Mattie Johnson, principal of Division High School. I met Mrs. Johnson when I was a graduate research assistant assigned to a project in the school in which she was an assistant principal. The first day of data collecting, I awoke to my doorbell, not to my alarm. My ride was there and I was still in bed. My colleagues left while I hurriedly threw on my clothes, raced for my car, and speeded to Newtown.

I arrived at the school 20 minutes late, embarrassed, flustered, and apologetic. Hoping to meet the other research assistants before having to face my interviewees, I rushed into the main office looking for a familiar face. A secretary, seeing my bewilderment, sought to help me. She directed me to the inner administrative offices. As I opened the door, I glimpsed a colleague. Just as I felt a wave of relief sweep over me, an imposing, regal woman stepped between us. Life all but drained from me. Before I could begin to apologize or explain, the woman grinned, then emitted a deep, hearty chuckle that made even me grin. Smiling with her whole being, she said, "You must be the one who overslept. I'm Mrs. Johnson, the Assistant Principal."

I tripped over my words, embarrassed and annoyed that my friends told her about my oversleeping; they could have been more discrete. I need not have worried, however, for Mrs. Johnson's reaction was accepting and understanding. She did not let me flounder. She put her hands on my shoulders, directing my face to hers, and said, "Honey, being late isn't the end of the world. Don't you worry about it. We're glad you're here and you're all right. Come into my office and catch your breath while I get you some coffee." She continued to put me at ease through stories she told about herself, stopping only when she felt I was composed and ready to begin my work. "Now," she said, "would you like to interview me?" Little did we know that this brief encounter would become the framework for many more interviews with her and her future school staff.

Mattie's sensitivity and warmth heightened my awareness of being cared for. I was conscious of her position of power and, at the same time, of how she treated me with dignity that enhanced my feeling of empowerment and my perception of her strength. Her reaching out to me opened a space where trust, respect, friendship, and collaboration could grow. I remember wondering what it would be like to work for/with such a principal and whether I, as a former administrator, had been as caring as she. Had I understood my power to be a vehicle for giving care, for establishing an environment where people learned how to trust, grow, and respect others in the community? Her actions prompted me to question school leadership and organization. What qualities lead to one's becoming a "caring" leader? How would that kind of leadership resonate with the staff? What kind of school organization is necessary to foster an ethic of caring? Was it possible for schools to be caring places? What were caring places?

That initial meeting with Mattie Johnson influenced my thinking over the next few years. The more I tried to envision schools as caring places, the more I questioned my understanding of the concept of caring. I read about it from the perspectives of psychologists (Baker Miller, 1976; Gilligan, 1982, 1983; Gilligan, Lyons, & Hanmer, 1990); philosophers (Noddings, 1984, 1988, 1991; Taylor et al., 1994); theologians (Buber, 1965; Macmurray, 1950); and sociologists (Bellah, Madsen, Sullivan, Swidler, & Tipton, 1985). From those works I began to understand what caring is and why it is so necessary to have it as a foundation for our schools. It is not just a "touchy-feely," sentimental concept, but it is "a requirement for the existence of human beings" (Baker Miller, 1976, p. 88); the basis for persons to realize freedom and genuine personhood (Macmurray, 1950); the cornerstone on which community is built and without which "the organic community disintegrates from within" (Buber, 1965, p. 197). Caring is about relationships—about *living in relation* to others; about *achieving personal freedom* by becoming "indissolubly linked" (Beck, 1992, p. 456) with those whose lives intersect with ours. I doubted that our schools encouraged our children—and our staffs—to see themselves in relation to others in order to become personally free.

THE NEED FOR SCHOOLS AS CARING PLACES

The concept of schools as caring places is not a new idea. With the growing concern among educators and the general public that our children are not learning what they need to know, came studies aimed at educational reform: The climate in schools needs to change; students are not "products" to be turned out; parents and students are not "clients" of the "corporation" of school. People who think and feel, and who do not leave their persona outside the school doors, constitute the places of schooling. Research shows that schools are failing students, particularly those from non-European and/or lower socioeconomic cultures, by not meeting their needs (Anyon, 1981, 1983; Apple, 1996; Cusick, 1983, 1992; Edelman, 1987; Fine, 1986, 1987; Ogbu, 1988; Olsen, 1988; Sedlak, Wheeler, Pullin, & Cusick, 1986; Weiler, 1988). Among the needs not met, identified by teachers, researchers, and social workers, are those of community, cultural understanding, and connectedness, none of which the organization of school supports, or it does so only in a limited way (Bryk, Lee, & Smith, 1990; Schorr, 1988). Additionally, reports on changing demographics in the United States to a "majority of minorities" (Hodgkinson, 1986) note the effects those changes may/will have on the kinds of schooling needed for children who are not members of the hegemonic society. Explicitly or implicitly, each account indicates the necessity for treating *all* youngsters with more caring and understanding, but especially those currently underserved in school systems.

From my experience as a teacher in poor urban and rural schools and as a researcher in urban schools, I questioned whether it was possible to create and nurture schools that functioned within an ethic of caring. There seemed to be three major stumbling blocks. First, an ethic of caring would have to grow from within an established bureaucratic hierarchy consisting of a profusion of power relationships. Caring, consequently, would have to be understood within a structure of power. Second, school as a caring place would suggest caring for a collective of persons and groups within the collective, not only caring between individuals. What would that entail? Furthermore, who would be responsible for the care of the institution, the community as a whole? Finally, an ethic of caring has been examined from a white, European perspective, with little or no acknowledgment of the potential for different perspectives and/or enactments of caring based on cultural backgrounds. A primary concern of educational reformers is restructured schools that better serve children who are not of the dominant group. Therefore, what considerations would be given to the cultural impact on the ways in which diverse persons within school communities perceive and enact caring behavior?

In this chapter, I present a short analysis of an ethic of caring, its characteristics, and how those characteristics are enacted to become caring. Following that discussion, I present considerations—particularly organizational and leadership changes—necessary for the nurturance of caring in an atmosphere supportive of a bureaucratic hierarchy.

TENETS OF AN ETHIC OF CARE

Feminist writers describe an ethic of care as a kind of moral reasoning. It takes on the qualities of connection, particularity of responsibility (the contextual), commitment, and reciprocity.

Connection

An ethic of care is a type of moral reasoning that is contingent on human relationships. It is "sustained by a morality that protects relationship—a morality whose essence lies in not abdicating responsibility, in not breaching primary loyalties, in not giving way to acrimony, in not deserting one another" (Gilligan, 1983, p. 33). An ethic of care implies connection, often described as a web or circle of relationships (Noddings, 1984), at its core. It is the development of interdependence rather than independence. Women, particularly, feel that responsibility to others in relation to self is of utmost importance. That often leads to dilemmas when women's needs are counter to those for whom they feel responsible, as they find it difficult to meet their own needs at the expense of others.

May Sarton (1978) beautifully illustrates the importance and tug of a web of relations on women's moral reasoning. In her book, *A Reckoning*, she follows a 60-year-old woman, Laura Spelman, from her being told she has inoperable cancer to her death. Laura, finding out she has a limited time to live, determines to die her own way, that is, to live only doing the consequential things in her life, and to do them as she chooses. Her initial reaction is not to tell her family until her physical health requires her to do so. She finds out, however, that all her decisions involving dying constitute a web of relationships that she cannot ignore: her children and her sisters, each seen as distinct individuals to be dealt with differently; her mother; and her maiden aunt. She also realizes that she cannot disregard the web that exists to connect her to nature and the environment. (See Noddings, 1984, 1992, for a discussion of human relationships to animals, the environment, and manufactured products.)

> Yes, Laura thought, it's like a web. Whatever the secret, the real connections, we are inextricably woven into a huge web together, and detaching the threads, one by one, is hideously painful. As long as one still feels the tug, one is not ready to die. . . . But, she reminded herself, the future is not my concern now. I have to shut it out. Only the present moment can have any real substance—so she looked again at the azalea and noted what unusually large single blossoms it had, and she felt that this looking, this still intense joy in a flower, was her way of praising God. Outside the human web, there was another far more complex

and yet not binding structure that included Grindle [her dog] and the azalea and she herself, and in that she could rest. (p. 183)

As Laura becomes progressively more ill and must be taken to the hospital, she finds that making connections with the strangers who "care" for her is immensely important.

By the time he was through this young man would know all about her years in the sanatorium, about her hysterectomy, and about her damaged lungs—and that is all he would know. Laura was amazed to discover that she was struggling to make a connection on another level. In a hospital one is reduced to being a body, one's history is the body's history, and perhaps that is why something deep inside a person reaches out, a little like a spider trying desperately to find a corner on which to begin to hang a web, the web of personal relations. (p. 204)

She attempts to converse with the young doctor. In the course of the conversation she tells him that she is dying. When his cajoling does not move Laura from the seriousness of her intended discussion with him, he rises from the chair telling her he must see several more patients. Laura's thoughts are, "Of course to do their work they couldn't afford to come in contact with a patient's soul. There was always that out" (p. 205).

Throughout the novel, Laura attempts to die as an individual not bound by others' wants and desires. However, she is unable to accomplish that, recognizing the needs of those within her web of relationships and her responsibilities to them. As Laura's cancer increasingly debilitates her, she says time and again that she must acknowledge her growing dependency on others. I disagree with Sarton's use of the term "dependency," for I think there was interdependence, as Laura's children and sisters continued to look to her for the strength they needed to come to terms with her dying. Laura was interdependent within a network of social relationships.

The young intern, however, is an example of independence and autonomy. He did not want to be drawn into a "real" relationship with Laura, even for a moment. His concern was to accomplish his job of taking three more medical histories before his round of duty ended, not to help a dying woman understand death.

A woman's connections to others, her circles of care, her web of relationships never leave her, even when she most thinks she wants them to. Within an ethic of care, connection is the center of moral reasoning. Her individuality often is subsumed in connection. Gilligan (1982) notes, however, that a woman achieves the highest level of moral reasoning when she is able to reflectively consider a situation and understand that there are times when she must care for herself first.

Particularity of Responsibilities

To reflectively consider each situation, that is, to study the particularity of context for each moral decision, is paramount to living by an ethic of care. Ubiquitous rules and principles do not apply, for caring is based in the specific context and in the concrete, not in the universal and abstract. Responsibilities and relationships, rather than rights and rules, are at its center. Each dilemma or condition determines the criteria for judgment, as labeling any specific act as universally or absolutely responsive to caring is impossible (Gilligan, 1982).

With each principle there is an exception. For example, one might hold the principle that abortion is wrong unless the mother's life is in danger. Consequently, the morality of rules and principles can be dangerous. Principles, furthermore, lend themselves to self-righteousness. Morality in an ethic of caring, therefore, is contextual, emerging as more details become known about a situation. The result is that an ethic of care based on individual human experiences is subject less and less to general rules and principles as more details are known about a situation, for "everyone wants to be received, to elicit a response that is congruent with an underlying need or desire" (Noddings, 1992, p. 17). An ethic of care suggests that although people may be in similar situations, they may choose different ways of handling their particular circumstances.

Let us return to Sarton's Laura to illustrate caring in context and not according to rules. Although Laura wanted to direct her dying to suit herself, she acknowledged that she needed to inform relatives sooner than she had intended because she realized they were a part of her dying. However, she wanted to inform them as she felt ready to deal with them on a deeply emotional level.

Her eldest sister, Jo, a highly successful academic, arrived unannounced. After many attempts to open the door to understand Jo, Laura finally asked:

> "Why did you come, Jo?"
> "After all, you are ill."
> " 'Families are different,' you said, earlier. And yet—forgive me for being blunt—you must have intimate friends who are far closer to you now than I. We haven't talked like this for years." Jo took a swallow of coffee and put the cup down. (p. 176)

"Caring" is quite different for Laura and for Jo. Jo lived by rules and principles. One of the principles was that "one should visit family when ill, and the ill member ought to wish to be visited" (p. 181). Jo could not respond to Laura's inquiry with any reason other than that Laura was family and there are certain expectations for all family members. If Jo had functioned within an ethic of care, she would have called to find out if she was welcome at that time. If Laura had declined her visit, Jo, from the standpoint of an ethic of care, would not have come, despite the universal expectations of family members in times of illness. She also would have tried to understand Laura's perspective on her own process of dying.

Perhaps a bit more difficult was Laura's "caring" situation with her doctor, whom she trusted and admired. The doctor had promised Laura that she would live to see the spring. Knowing how agonizing the hospital stay had been for her, the doctor arranged for her son to carry her to the chaise in the garden after her return home. Laura, too weak and sick, no longer wanted to leave her bed. The doctor, however, neglected to see that, for he wanted to keep his promise to her; keeping promises is an important principle. Only after Laura had a severe coughing attack that weakened her even further could the doctor see that he had not shown care. An ethic of caring provides no set of principles, no recipe, for care. Caring is grounded in the daily experiences and moral problems of real people; it is a way of being in relation (Gilligan, 1982; Noddings, 1984; Tronto, 1987, 1993).

Commitment

Commitment is most important in an ethic of caring. The commitment spoken of is not that one will be forever present in body to the other, but that there is a joint "knowing" or awareness of caring between people. Caring involves "a commitment that is stronger than the desire to run" (Beck, 1992); it requires devotion, loyalty (Noddings, 1984). The caring relationship may change over time, but the bond remains. The form of caring or the circumstances may alter, but the fact that one cares, that one is devoted, does not.

The longer one is committed to caring, accepting that it demands responsibility, the more potential there is that one will have to sacrifice. Sacrifice, ultimately, enhances the experience of the one making it. Gilligan (1982) and Noddings (1984) suggest that women commit themselves to caring and are willing to deny themselves in order to care for others. Their self-denial, however, is devalued by a patriarchal society that prizes individual actions leading to accomplishment more than it does nurturing (Beck, 1992).

Reciprocity—Giving and Receiving

In order for a caring relationship to be complete, both care-giving and care-receiving are necessary (Noddings, 1984). Attending to the one receiving care, and understanding the care-receiver's needs and desires from the latter's perspective (motivational displacement), distinguish the care-giver. As long as caring occurs—from moments to long durations of time—the care-giver really sees, hears, and feels what the other wants to convey. From that concentrated attention, she understands what the care-receiver imparts and she responds in a way that enhances the other's goals or objectives. For reciprocity to occur, the receiver acknowledges receipt of the care offered, and the care-giver, in turn, accepts the care-receiver's gift of responsiveness.

Reciprocity is called into question when the care offered is not consistent with the care-receiver's needs or wants. Noddings maintains that it is still possible to have a fulfilled caring relationship in some circumstances. If the relationship must be maintained because of formal or long-term expectations (parent/child, teacher/student, doctor/patient), the cared-for must respond to the care-giving through respect and obedience, thus sustaining a reciprocal relationship of caring.

If, however, the motives of care are actually such that the care-giver wants or needs to be cared-for, the care-receiver is in an intolerable position. The care-giver in that situation demands response from the care-receiver to satisfy her own needs. The one cared-for, thus, becomes the care-giver, for she has been put in the position of considering the needs and motives of the one caring. Alternatively, she "becomes an ethical hero—one who behaves as though cared-for without the sustenance of caring" (Noddings, 1984, p. 76). That is, the care-receiver affects being cared for out of concern for the other in order to allow the care-giver to receive the kind of caring she requires at that time. If the cared-for interprets each of the care-giver's acts as sincere offerings of caring, then the cared-for assumes a legitimacy for the care-giver's inability to interpret her needs. Thus, the care-receiver acknowledges receipt of care, and therefore of the other's position as the one caring.

To illustrate the reciprocity of care, let me again turn to Laura and the people who intended to be care-givers to her. As Laura grew weaker, she experienced a need to have someone sit with her. Mary, the woman hired to help her, was experienced in taking care of dying persons. She understood Laura's need and offered to stay in the room with her. Mary's caring was to bring her mending and to sit unobtrusively, not talking, but responding to Laura according to the latter's needs. Laura rejoiced in that care. Caring was reciprocal in the way Laura took Mary's hand or smiled at her when she sat quietly doing her work.

Laura's children, however, continually wanted to be with Laura, to talk with her, and to *do for her*. Their "offers" of care were really efforts to be cared-for; they needed her dependence on them in order to feel they were doing something to help her through her illness. Laura's first response was annoyance and anger that they were *not* caring for her. After reflecting on her position and theirs, she became, in Noddings's term, the ethical heroine. She accepted and took responsibility for the care offered and responded to her children as the one cared-for. She allowed her youngest son to sit with her and initiated conversation when she knew he was uncomfortable in the silence. She, beyond the need or desire for such things, genuinely responded to her daughter's need to play the guitar and sing *for* her. All the while, Laura was conscious of the relationship and how she was responding. The critical point is that she sought to maintain the relationships, seeing the intended care-givers in the best light possible.

The above is the fundamental basis on which feminist thinkers and educational reformers wish to change organizational theory and leadership in order for schools and other institutions in society to become caring places. I based my discussion of an ethic of care on my understanding of the works of prominent feminist thinkers. Note that the emphasis was on the individual's caring for another individual. Schooling, however, involves caring not only between individuals, but for a *collection* of individuals, for the school community as a whole. It is necessary, therefore, to examine the structure of organization from the perspective of the whole in order to think about creating a climate that is supportive of an ethic of caring as the basis for school reform efforts.

RECONCEPTUALIZING ORGANIZATION
AND LEADERSHIP FOR CARING

Prior to beginning this study, I thought about present school organization, hierarchical by design and in operation—a bureaucracy. Bureaucracy is driven by rules and norms, ostensibly to maintain or increase efficiency, but that in essence function to preserve the structure by restricting the range of options for all but those at the top (Kanter, 1977). The result is the maintenance of inequality within the organization, as well as in society.

> As both a structure and a process, bureaucracy must be located within its social context; in our society, that is a context in which social relations between classes, races, and sexes are fundamentally unequal. Bureaucracy, as the "scientific organization of inequality," serves as a filter for these other forms of domination, projecting them into an institutional arena that both rationalizes and maintains them. (Ferguson, 1984, pp. 7–8)

Organizational systems become analytical and defining, driven by the desire to be technically well-functioning wholes. To accomplish such goals, there is a need to analyze, understand, and explain by breaking down the system into its component parts and defining each of the parts in turn (Schaef, 1985). Jobs become organizational aspects to be defined apart from the whole and independent from the people who fill them. Personal relationships have little importance in hierarchical structures.

Extrapolating this critique of bureaucracy in general to that of schooling, I believe it would be accurate to say that the bureaucracy of schooling is a political tool to maintain and further the interests of the dominant class; that it has not been conceptualized as a "tool for the pursuit of personal, group, or class interests" (Fischer & Sirianni, 1984, p. 11); and that it is a tool of "power over," limiting and/or negating the value of connection, interdependence, particularity, context, and, ultimately, caring within community. For those reasons, a strand of educational reformers and feminist thinkers propose an ethic of caring as the basis for school reorganization and leadership

Feminist scholars emphasize reconceptualizing organizational theory and give impetus to the creation and realization of a climate supporting an ethic of caring as a means of perceiving school reform as more than tinkering. It is to think differently about the structure of society and about the distribution of power. Feminist scholars advocate the creation of structural models that would support and sustain community, connection, interdependence, and commitment among all persons within an institution. Hierarchies would be flattened and leadership would emanate from the center, constructing a web of interconnections between and among the various groupings within schools; administrators would be part of the work schematic, and teachers, students, and staff would be part of the leadership (Acker, 1991; Beck, 1992, 1994; Calas & Smircich, 1988; Hearn, Sheppard, Tancred-Sheriff, & Burrell, 1989; Kanter, 1977; Smircich, 1985). An ethic of care would alter significantly the power structure of schooling, which, in turn, would affect that of society in general.

Leadership in organizations that stressed caring would of necessity have to change. No longer would it be sufficient to manage and control solely from a top-down perspective, nor would it be enough for one person to be the decision-maker. Caring leadership would entail becoming a *co*-worker, that is, working *with* the other members of the organization; sharing decision-making and responsibilities; envisioning leadership from the center of an organization, not from the top; and allowing co-workers to work from their positions of strength in order to contribute effectively to the organization, and to *take responsibility* for their work (Beck & Murphy, 1994; Blackmore, 1991a, 1991b, 1993; Block, 1993; Regan, 1990; Regan & Brooks, 1995; Reiger, 1993; Smircich & Morgan, 1982). Leaders would encourage and value cooperation as much as competition, interdependence as much as independence, and the situational and contextual as well as the generalizable.

Yet, little that I observed and experienced in schools evidenced such organization and leadership. Schools reflected a top-down model of authority. Nona Lyons's (1990) inquiry into the way administrators handle ethical dilemmas illustrates such a model. In her study, she describes the traditional bureaucracy based on notions of justice, reciprocity, and contract. Obligation or duty, and an underlying concern with equality, fairness, and hierarchy in interactions, drive the relationships. Administrators in that tradition are autonomous, defining precisely the contractual terms between the corporation and the teachers and staff; they are expected to act fairly and to argue in favor of, and persuasively for, the institution; and they are to predict with reasonable accuracy the outcomes of conflict. Additionally, bureaucratic practices of limiting information and communication to only information necessary for the teachers' specific roles in the schools produce isolation, depersonalization, and alienation. The results are deskilling, fragmented lives, and the loss of connection with other human beings. Teachers view only the work in their individual classrooms and the success or failure of their students. Instructors have little or no understanding of how their work integrates with that of others in the overall goals of the school or with education initiatives on a larger scale. In general, teachers have limited knowledge about each step in the process necessary to reach institutional goals.

Of significance to me was the failure of the literature to address the issue of creating an ethic of caring within the established bureaucratic hierarchy. Revolution is not likely. Therefore, those committed to reform of organization and leadership need to understand how such reconceptualizations would fit into the current power structures, adapting and massaging them as climates of caring developed and strengthened. Although many feminists discussed reorganization and leadership necessary to create institutions that are caring places, there was no empirical work examining the creation of caring between a leader and the constituents of an organization. My study, therefore, focuses on organizational structure as it is embedded in a framework of power, as well as on those within the organization who bring histories of experiences with, and expectations of, power relationships to their work.

CONCLUSION

Initially, I intended to examine the perceptions and experiences of Division High School's administrators and staff as they participated in site-based management, a leadership style focused on developing collaboration and cooperation among and between those groups. Since the goals were consistent with those embodied in an ethic of caring, I wanted to ascertain whether the school community thought in terms of caring, how they would define it, and how they envisioned developing their school as a caring place.

As I interviewed teachers and administrators, I changed the focus of my question to the *relationship* between caring and power. Virtually all the participants talked about the need for a caring environment, but the understandings and perceptions varied widely concerning the comprehension of what caring meant to them individually, as groups, and as a whole staff. What one person defined as caring, another perceived as control, an oppressive use of power.

The principal's actions began to evoke discomfort in me. Despite the many instances of concern and compassion that she proferred various faculty members and students, I observed her using the power of her position in ways that angered and alienated individuals. I struggled to make sense of her caring, for she, indeed, seemed to have a driving passion for the school as a whole and the community of individuals within it. Time and again she remarked to me that she had to consider the "big picture," implying that it was her responsibility to care for the school by making sure that all aspects "fit" together for the good of the community. I began to question the understanding of caring in reference to a leader caring for a group, rather than caring for individuals. In spite of explications of and references to caring, theoretical and research literature provided no analysis of caring in terms of a collective. Feminists (Gilligan, 1982; Gilligan, Lyons, & Hanmer, 1990; Noddings, 1984, 1992; Regan, 1990; Regan & Brooks, 1995) seemed to assume that caring between individuals would serve as a template for caring for the group. As the study evolved, I began to question whether it would.

Consideration of caring within a framework of power evoked yet another puzzle for me. I had tended to view caring and power as two separate concepts, the former, "good," and the latter, "bad." Listening and observing at Division caused me to doubt the dichotomy I had assumed existed between them as they affected school organization and leadership. I also questioned the reality of a dichotomy between caring and power in my own life. Both of those insights lead me to posit a potential change in the theoretical basis of caring: Could power be used to effect acts of caring? Did caring require power? What was the *link* between caring and power that enhanced the effectiveness of caring? The nature of the interrelationship of caring and power, not the dichotomy, ultimately became my undertaking. I needed to determine what caring in a framework of power "looked like" in order to understand a "caring power."

For organizational structure to change, school leaders would need to possess the vision and power to facilitate the necessary reorganization. This type of leadership, however, would be expected to occur within a framework of bureaucratic hierarchy. Although feminists are redefining leadership and power, Nona Lyons (1990) pointedly noted that "they have not demonstrated empirically how their model actually works" (p. 279). My hope was to find this model of school as a caring place, one in which power enhanced caring. I hoped to see a school transformed into a caring institution, but I was unsure of what caring *looked* like.

CHAPTER 2

From the Individual to the Collective: An Ethic of Caring in the Organization of School

Feminist scholars have given impetus to the need to create organizational structures and leadership styles based on an ethic of caring. From educational research we have learned that caring is integral to the schooling of all children, but specifically for children of cultures other than white, European, and middle class (Bryk, Lee, & Smith, 1990; Edelman, 1987; Schorr, 1988). To effect caring in schools, educators and policy makers need to reconceptualize the societal order and the distribution of power, for the creation of schools as caring places would alter significantly the power relations in such schools and, consequently, in the larger community.

Efficiencies, rights, individualism, abstraction, and generalities ground the current bureaucratic hierarchy of schools. In contrast, those who advocate organizational and leadership praxis that is influenced by tenets of an ethic of caring emphasize quite different principles: particulars, responsibilities, connectedness, the concrete, and context (Fox-Genovese, 1991; Gilligan, 1982, 1983; Grimshaw, 1986; Noddings, 1984, 1992). It is reasonable to surmise that nurturing an ethic of caring within structures that are bureaucratic and hierarchical could be a complex, if not daunting, task. Additionally, caring on an institutional level, I believe, requires recognition of the collective. That is, caring, most often conceptualized in terms of the individual, must be reconceptualized from the perspective of caring for and about the whole. As the basis for organizational and leadership transformation, an ethic of caring becomes politically charged because of potential shifts in power relationships.

To examine caring from an institutional perspective, I consider the caring ethic from the positions of organizational and leadership initiatives as they specifically affect schooling. I conclude with the suggestion that attempts to create an ethic of caring within bureaucratic organizations become a politics of caring, an integration of caring and power.

18

CRITIQUE OF AN ETHIC OF CARING

In this section, I examine specific aspects of an ethic of caring from a feminist perspective and use them to question organizational and leadership revision within a framework of care. School leaders consider an ethic of caring from the perspective of individual caring, that is, what a person needs to know and do in order to be a caring person. As a school reform measure, however, an ethic of caring requires a vision of "collective" effort, involving support and resources that individual persons either could not provide or could provide only on a limited basis.

Within the context of a school, it is necessary to consider changes in leadership and organization needed to provide a climate conducive to caring for a community of persons. Several points deserve attention.

1. What is caring from an institutional perspective?
2. Whose—administrators', teachers', students', parents'—caring will it be?
3. Will organization and leadership designed for nurturing a climate of caring maintain the dominant interests, or replace one form of oppression with another?
4. What effect would the concept of a "caring power" have on school as a bureaucratic hierarchy?

An "ethic" of caring contemplated from those perspectives quickly becomes a "politics" of caring. To explore more fully the "collectivity" of caring and its link with power, I discuss caring as (1) women's work, (2) connection, (3) community, and (4) reciprocity. Throughout, I attempt to show the need to move beyond an understanding of caring between individuals to that between a leader and her constituents.

Caring as Women's Work

Feminist scholars and educational researchers and policy makers write about the need to re-vision our social institutions so that the organization and leadership style encourage caring among community members (Beck, 1992, 1994; Beck & Murphy, 1994; Blackmore, 1991a; Calas & Smircich, 1988; Enomoto, 1995, 1996; Ferguson, 1984; Marshall, 1992; Marshall & Rusch, 1996; Regan & Brooks, 1995; Rusch & Marshall, 1995). The rationale for their work derives from the notion that communities need to engender relationships of caring. They base their work largely on the history and tradition of females as caregivers. Because of their experiences as women, female scholars ground their work in the belief that they *know* what caring is (Fisher & Tronto, 1990;

Nunner-Winkler, 1993). Additionally, those women draw on psychological data that support the notion that women see themselves in relation to others, that is, in positions to serve others or as having primary responsibility to and for others (Baker Miller, 1976; Gilligan, 1982, 1983). Psychologists attribute the latter not to natural instinct, but to socialization (Baker Miller, 1976; Chodorow, 1978). Although many feminist writers hesitate to call it a "female" ethic of caring, the implication is that it is easier for women to care than men (Baker Miller, 1976; Gilligan, 1982; Noddings, 1984, 1992; Tronto, 1987, 1993).

Feminists suggest that women's lives provide the space to question traditional values, which often are viewed as partriarchal. Among those questioned are values that portray human lives as dispensable in the service of abstract ideas or causes; those that depict caring for others or devoting one's life to serving others as relatively unimportant; and those that characterize the responsibilities of maintaining human life and nurturing connections as sharply distinct from, and inferior to, the affairs of the public world (Arendt, 1958; Grimshaw, 1986; Tronto, 1993).

Caring continues to be devalued, despite the recognition that "human existence requires care from others and such caring is an important part of life" (Fisher & Tronto, 1990, p. 35). Caring is denigrated because it is associated with women's work, which, ultimately, continues to be relegated to the private sphere of society (Brown, 1982; Elshtain, 1981; Finch & Groves, 1983; Graham, 1983; Hartsock, 1984; Jaggar, 1983; Tronto, 1987, 1989, 1993). As such, it has virtually no place in the description of the "good life" that provides the focus for Western philosophy—autonomous, rational, and public (Fisher & Tronto, 1990).

Focus in caring is on the care-giver rather than on the act of caring. Caring conceptualized in that manner maintains modern societies' world vision of a gendered division of labor. Men are autonomous and rational and motivated to accomplish purposeful, formal, and paid activities in the public domain. Women are dependent and caring, ministering to the needs of family, and building and maintaining relationships, unpaid in the household. In other words, there is a public and private division in society evidenced by "men-who-do" and "women-who-care" (Graham, 1983, p. 23). That sets up a dichotomy, determining what counts as "caring" by who does it as much as by what is done. Such a dichotomy, in turn, contributes to primary defining characteristics of women's and men's self-identity and work: Women are "caring," and men are "not-caring"; women are to focus on others, and men are to focus on themselves (Baker Miller, 1976; Graham, 1983).

Conceptualizing an ethic of caring within such a dichotomy makes one pause to question the nurturance that can take place in relationships that are not intimate or private. That is, if caring is separate from the public world, how does one perceive nurturing in terms of broad educational policy? Can women remain "unchanged" as they function in the public world? Should they? There is also the danger in such a polarization of simply substituting one oppressive form of dominance with another. If males are seen as "naturally" corrupt, and females as "virtuous," will persons espousing an ethic of caring attempt to reverse the current oppressors and oppressed?

Some feminists interpret women's propensity for caring not as a genetic trait, but as one that is socially constructed (Chodorow, 1978; Gilligan, 1982; Noddings, 1984). They view it as a positive dimension in their lives, despite its devaluation by the patriarchal structure of society. Others, however, view the relationship between women and caring as oppressive because of its complexity. Emphasis is put on the psychological aspects of caring—connection, relationship, interdependence, commitment, and community. Yet, little consideration is given to the fact that caring is often time-consuming, difficult, and unpleasant. Additionally, to effect a caring act frequently requires collaboration with others rather than functioning autonomously, the more valued behavior in the public sphere (Fisher & Tronto, 1990; Ungerson, 1983). In the patriarchal family, caring is reduced to an obligatory transaction of goods and services, leaving women defined in terms of female sacrifice and supreme selflessness (Graham, 1983). In the marketplace, women are expected to care for their families, yet are devalued when they do. Consider the following.

The United States Congress passed the Family and Medical Leave Act, legislation designed to allow males and females unpaid leave to care for family medical needs ("Family Leave," 1993). Created to protect people from losing their jobs in times of family medical emergencies or births/adoptions, the act has accomplished its intent only in part. Men rarely reduce their working hours or take leave to help their families because employers do not view those who take advantage of this act as serious about their work. Consequently, women continue to be the primary leave-takers in order to care for family needs. There is mounting evidence that employers are choosing not to hire women or are finding reasons to sever employment when women take extended leave (Stahl, 1993), resulting in small employers being "less likely to employ women of child-bearing years and more likely to cut the number of low-skilled jobs" (Mary Reed, quoted in "Family Leave," 1993, p. A3).

It is difficult for caring to be a *collective* effort when the public sphere does not value caring. The marketplace discourages role reversal, that is, making home and family a *family* priority, but encourages females to give priority to home responsibilities (Ungerson, 1983). Doing so is a way of returning women to the home and, therefore, reclaiming the public domain solely for males.

Caring as a collective effort is problematic. Our societal norms reflect an attitude of: women "care" and men "do." Arendt (1958) pointed out that in the prepolitical society of Greece, home was the place to which men returned to revitalize themselves after the challenges of public life. Such an attitude exists in the United States today. Women are expected to forge and maintain the connections within the family. Through those strong connections of caring, however, dependency results, not because women receive care, but because they give care (Graham, 1983). If women can be convinced it is their responsibility to be the primary—or sole—care-givers, the public domain will remain male-dominated and controlled, thereby keeping women from making significant progress in public life. The result is women's continued dependency on men.

An ethic of caring, however, presumes an integration of men into women's caring work, thus making caring as valuable as other activities. It requires that the "worthiness" (Fisher & Tronto, 1990, p. 36) of caring be recognized. That presumes that those who traditionally have relegated caring to life's private domain desire to recognize it as essential to the public domain. Reworking schools to become places that are caring communities "is dependent on a *transforming*, and on a challenging of the sharp distinction between a public and a private ethic" (Grimshaw, 1986, p. 203, emphasis in original). The question becomes, is there a tension of new needs that is great enough to motivate people for change, however painful? If not, change is unlikely, for "a transvaluation of values can only be accomplished when there is a tension of new needs and a new set of needy people who feel all old values as painful although they are not conscious of what is wrong" (Daly, 1973, quoted in Grimshaw, 1986, p. 155). For caring to become collective, men, as well as women, must feel a need for interdependence and connection that causes tension with the current necessity for independence and autonomy. Change, however, does not necessarily come with its recognition. Change may lead to ignoring the "oppressive and oppression-linked" (Grimshaw, 1986, p. 36) aspects of caring and serve to reinforce what is already perceived as women's work. An ethic of caring may strengthen the current structure. In schools, more females may be "awarded" positions as principals to administer acts of caring determined by male superiors. Will the position of principal, then, become devalued in the long term?

Concern over the potential to devalue principals committed to an ethic of caring is particularly poignant at this time. There is asymmetry between responsibility and power, not only between positions in institutional hierarchies, but between males and females in the same or similar positions, and between care-givers and care-receivers. In the case of principals, where responsibility is great, but power is limited, will females, more than males, be expected to compensate for the deficiencies in the caring process? Will female principals be given the "toughest" schools—those with the least resources and those needing the most care—and be expected to accomplish as much or more because they are encouraged—perhaps, mandated—to create a caring atmosphere that is monitored through bureaucratic practices?

Caring as Connection

Connection serves to balance extreme individualism and autonomy. Relationships are essential to living fully as a human being and to developing viable communities. But there is also a negative side to connectedness. Seeing oneself only in relation to others is problematic because connection may be a way of promoting illusory expectations or a way of escaping from old forms of coercion and constraint only to fall into new ones (Grimshaw, 1986).

An ethic of caring within schools would have the potential of giving women the illusion of power while continuing to oppress them. Those in power positions, usually males, may agree to the need for caring within their schools. Rather than integrating themselves into the work of caring, they may pander to the women's egos as "natural" care-givers. Female teachers and/or administrators, understanding the importance of caring and willing to work at it regardless of the time and effort required,[2] are delighted that males finally are recognizing their contributions to society. Men, on the other hand, will be the "doers" because they got the job done, that is, they made the decisions to implement an ethic of caring and saw that others, often women, accomplished the tasks.

Women may become inextricably connected to others, unable to separate themselves from the act of caring. The latter may result in caring becoming a burden, done out of obligation in order to meet socially constructed norms, one of which is woman as care-giver (Fisher & Tronto, 1990; Ungerson, 1983). Meeting those norms may even be done in self-defense; that is, if women do not conform to the expectations set for them, the assumption is that something is "wrong" with them. Women are expected to care, to live their lives in connection with others. If they do not, they are selfish, self-centered, or out of sync with society's norms; there is something wrong, not with the system, but with the women.

Not living up to the family's and society's expectations of connection implies not difference, but deviance or inferiority. Therefore, women often feel compelled to make choices regarding who they are. They often are pressured to stop caring for themselves in order to maintain their private relationships within the family and, therefore, maintain respect in the public sphere. Women are asked to sacrifice themselves to fit the norms of the larger society.

People of non-European backgrounds and heritages are subject to pressure from the hegemonic society to assimilate into the dominant culture. Studies conducted by Ogbu (1988), Olsen (1988), and Peshkin and White (1990) show the harsh realities students of color experience when they do not meet the expectations of the white middle class. In virtually all cases, not meeting hegemonic standards implies not difference, but deviance or inferiority. Therefore, those persons often deny their own culture's strong valuation of caring in order to become "connected" to the dominant society. Like women, they are asked to sacrifice themselves to fit the norms of the hegemony.

Will an ethic of caring be used to allow administrators and teachers, majority and minority peoples, to uncover the now unspoken grievances against one another? Or will the web of relationships justify relationships that perpetuate inequality, thus preventing caring? Will an ethic of caring become the rationale for developing hatred and dislike of differences?

> Within a framework of inequality the existence of conflict is denied and the means to engage openly in conflict are excluded. Further, inequality itself creates additional factors that skew any interaction and prevent open engagement around real differences. Instead, inequality generates hidden conflict around elements that the inequality itself has set in motion. In sum, both sides are diverted from open conflict around falsifications. For this hidden conflict, there are no acceptable social forms or guides because this conflict supposedly doesn't exist. (Baker Miller, 1976, p. 13)

An ethic of caring presumes connections, but perhaps those connections may be forged only through "caring conflicts." There is little to suggest that an ethic of caring as an educational reform measure provides for concrete thought about relationships between and among teachers, administrators, and other staff members. Such relationships require caring on a *collective* basis, as well as on an individual one. As a foundation for reform, it needs to be thought of from the perspective of groups of people within a school, as well as the entire population of a school.

Living in connection also can mean living through another, not living one's own life, but a Quixotic existence. Grimshaw (1986) describes this kind of connectedness as "mapping" others' needs and feelings, as one understands them, onto oneself and trying to identify with them. She uses as an example a wife who lives through her husband, therefore connecting with him. To her detriment—and his—she denies her own existence. Caring becomes self-sacrifice rather than self-fulfillment.

Psychological data also suggest that women may find satisfaction only in activities they can rationalize as serving others. Jean Baker Miller (1976) forcefully indicated the degree to which that occurs, saying that "many women truly cannot *tolerate or allow themselves* to feel that their life activities are for themselves" (p. 62, emphasis in original). Thus, they spend their lives finding ways to translate their own motivations into means of serving others. They believe that by devoting their lives to serving others, they will be loved and respected. The result is often the reverse: Others resent their super-human efforts, feeling trapped and controlled. Connectedness, in that sense, becomes power, a power that controls and manipulates others.

Exploring caring as control, Grimshaw (1986) referred to R. D. Laing's

Sanity, Madness, and the Family.[3] Through her discussion of this study, Grimshaw pointed out the dark side of connectedness.

> The mothers described in *Sanity, Madness, and the Family* are "connected" to their daughters, in that they see them simply as a projection of a family "phantasy" or of their own beliefs and desires. They are also unable to imagine or conceive of the "separateness" of their daughters. . . . The result of this was that, far from being able to "empathize" with their daughters, the mothers showed an almost total inability to understand what they were thinking and feeling. (pp. 181, 182)

Part of being connected is to be separate from. Unlike the dichotomy of connectedness and separateness that feminists often use to describe human relationships, care for others requires understanding oneself and having the ability to distinguish "self" from "other." To be able to care is to know oneself, to understand where oneself begins and ends in order not to see others as a "projection of self, or self as a continuation of the other" (Grimshaw, 1986, p. 183). To care is to relate and to separate simultaneously (Arendt, 1958). On the other hand, an unclear or idealized vision of connectedness can lead to coerciveness and the denial of the needs of individuals to forge their own paths and to develop their own understandings and goals (Grimshaw, 1986).

In a passage from "In and out of Harm's Way," Frye (1983) describes "the loving eye" as being separate from the one she cares about and for. Caring occurs because she knows herself and knows that she will see the other with her own eye.

> The loving perceiver can see without the presupposition that the other poses a constant threat or that the other exists for the seer's service; nor does she see with the other's eye instead of her own. Her interest does not blend the seer and the seen. . . . One who sees with a loving eye is separate from the other whom she sees. There are boundaries between them; she and the other are two. . . . The loving eye is one that pays a certain sort of attention. This attention can require a discipline *but* [emphasis in original] not a self-denial. The discipline is one of self-knowledge, knowledge of the scope and boundary of the self. What is required is that one know what are one's interests, desires and loathings, one's projects, hungers, fears and wishes, and that *one know what is and what is not determined by these* [emphasis added]. In particular, it is a matter of being able to tell one's own interests from those of others and of knowing where one's self leaves off and another begins. (pp. 74, 75)

The focus of an ethic of caring in schools is usually on caring for students, which is as it should be. But teachers need to understand themselves, their "scope and boundary," before they can begin to deal with the culture, values, and life-styles the children bring to their classes. If the staff is not reflective about themselves and what they believe, it does not seem likely that they will be reflective about the differences their students present. Understanding of self is necessary for a principal in order to lead staff to reflect on not only their individual selves, but their collective selves and how the latter affect the goals, organization, and interactions within the school.

In a classic longitudinal study of social class and teacher expectations, Ray Rist (1970) found that a kindergarten teacher's expectations affected the academic placement of her students, not only in kindergarten, but in each succeeding year. Some of these children were irreparably hurt academically because they did not meet the teacher's dress, language, or hygiene expectations. Her expectations were based not on "objective" evidence, but on her background, experiences, and life-style, all of which contributed to her idea of what a "good" student should be.

Teachers of the dominant culture may not be able to separate themselves from their students, resulting in an inability to perceive the value in their students' differences. An ethic of caring as the basis for schooling will require providing opportunities for staff members to connect with themselves and to see themselves as separate from each other and from their students. Only when they are able to see the students as different from themselves, can they begin to care. However, will there be support, that is, time and money, for the nurturance of teachers and administrators to reflect on their own and their collective values?

Caring as Community

Community is closely aligned to connection. Some educational reformers believe that building community within and around schools is a necessity if our schools are to survive and students are to benefit from them (Boyer, 1995; Goodlad, 1988, 1990; Holmes Group, 1986, 1988; Noddings, 1992).

Community, as well as an ethic of caring, arises from a web—or circles—of relationships, that is, relationships that extend from those most intimate to us to those we do not know yet. Noddings (1984) points out that there comes a point at which "an ethic of caring limits our obligation to those so far removed from us that completion (of caring) is impossible" (p. 152). Two salient points in regard to caring from a distance emerge. The first relates to caring for students. Noddings (1992) indicates that students do not necessarily belong in the most intimate circle, but still are in a relationship to the teacher that, ideally, is close. However, will teachers whose students are *not* of their own backgrounds, cultures, and values be able to relate closely to them? Or will the teachers, using an ethic of caring as a basis by which to "address the next circle and entreat aid," find an excuse for continuing not to address the needs of children to whom they do not instinctively relate, hoping that some "other" teacher or staff person will take up the job? This dilemma brings us to the second point, which returns us to a topic introduced earlier—the extent to which the boundaries of caring should be enlarged.

Realistically, we do not care equally for all people. We care most for those with whom we have much in common emotionally, physically, and/or culturally because it is "natural" and comfortable. We can relate to like people with little, if any, effort. If connection and preserving a web of relationships is fundamental to an ethic of caring, there is little basis for critical reflection on whether those relationships are good, healthy, or worth saving, because we begin with *our own* webs, those we already have accepted as good and worthy. An ethic of caring, then, "could become a defense of caring only for one's own family, friends, group, nation. From this perspective, caring could become a justification for any set of conventional relationships" (Tronto, 1987, pp. 659–660). By not reflecting on the connections, we may allow dislike and hatred of differences to grow.

As educational policy makers continue their work on the transformation of schools into caring places, it is imperative that they consider caring in terms of staff needs and education, and from a greater perspective than that of the individual. If an ethic of caring is modeled and practiced as Noddings (1984, 1992) suggests, then it seems reasonable to expect that teachers, administrators, and other staff will have to know how to care for *each other*; they will have to know how to model caring to persons not of their own cultures and values; *they*, perhaps, will need to be taught.

The notion of building community in schools raises issues that are often contradictory, especially concerning individualism and connection. In recent years, there has been much emphasis on altering schools and curriculum to encourage and support females and minorities to recognize their *individuality* and to reach their *individual* potentials. If community building becomes the focus, what will it take to resolve the dilemma of maintaining a clear sense of one's own identity and individualism while concurrently embedding it in relationships with others (Fox-Genovese, 1991; Grimshaw, 1986)? If a school's vision of connectedness is ambiguous or idealized, will the expectations for community or for harmony among the people within it be unrealistic? If so, will there be denial of the needs of others to "forge their own path and develop their own understanding and goals" (Grimshaw, 1986, p. 183)? Ultimately, will there be a loss of individuality?

Finally, there is the issue of self-interest and altruism related to the formation of a caring community. As background, consider Fox-Genovese's (1991) discussion of women and community. Women's commitment to building community is associated with their tendency to define themselves in relation to others and in the particular, rather than in the individual and abstract. Ironically, however, women's experience historically has been in individualistic societies and cultures, in other words, in unique family communities. Although they were excluded from public life and its achievement values of individualism, women quite possibly achieved empowerment from their ascribed position—that of creating a sense of belonging and bonding—within families, the basic units of communities. By so doing, they chanced constructing a "sentimental" (p. 39) understanding of community. That perception of community, then, becomes internal to the motivations and identities of the participants—a product of their commitment. It differs "from a more instrumental or contractual view of community in attributing affiliation to benevolence or even identity rather than to instrumental self-interest" (pp. 39–40).

In modern society, women are strongly encouraged to be the care-givers. The question is, do women work at building community from altruism, or from self-interest, seeking empowerment by meeting the expectations of the "ascriptive values of the community" (Fox-Genovese, 1991, p. 45)? Or, perhaps from both? Returning to a question posed earlier, is it possible for women to remain "unchanged" as they enter the public sphere?

Building community may be done solely out of self-interest. An ethic of caring, implemented for political purposes, may be used to further self-interest under the guise of creating community when, in fact, it becomes a means for furthering one's own interests and ideologies. Claims of caring may be used ideologically in order to mask more fundamental objectives. Consider union activities. Some local teachers' unions have set a cap on the number of students who can be enrolled in a class. On the one hand, this is a caring act, both for the students and for the teachers. Students learn better when there are fewer in the class, and teachers can devote more time to each student. There are instances, however, when teachers *choose* to allow additional students into the class. An example is a student who will stay in school if allowed to enroll in a particular teacher's class (Freedman, 1990). Another example is the enrollment of two additional students to all teachers' classes in a school where the absentee rate for classes is a fourth to a third. That would free teachers to hold in-school suspension, thus keeping students in school rather than sending them home or, more likely, out on the streets. I question whether the union is considering the students' interests, that is, caring for students, or is more concerned about maintaining its power within the bureaucracy. Perhaps we need to examine whether the claims or accusations of failure to care are actually diversions from injustices and oppression that plague us, or ways to conceal intentions—gaining power, for instance—that have nothing to do with care (Grimshaw, 1986).

In modern society where there is tension between the sensed need for community and the strong tradition of individualism (Bellah et al., 1985), it is possible for "community" to be created to serve the bureaucracy's own needs. That is done by using the rhetoric of an ethic of caring that those at the base of the "broken triangle" (McIntosh, 1983)[4]—women, minorities, the working class, and the poor—want to hear. The probability that the political process that creates bureaucracy will define what will be cared about and will tailor caring to meet the continued and changing needs, including self-perpetuation, of the institution of schooling is strong (Fisher & Tronto, 1990). An ethic of caring could become simply another tool to maintain a rule-bound, bureaucratic organizational structure and leadership within schools, and to maintain the current inequality that permeates and governs the larger society.

Caring as Reciprocal

Noddings discusses the importance of reciprocity in caring, saying that the caring relationship is incomplete if the one cared-for is unable to receive care from the one caring. Additionally, the one caring needs to know that her care-giving has been received, thus making the relationship reciprocal, with each person receiving as well as giving.

From a bureaucratic standpoint, however, what the care-giver has in her power to give and what the care-receiver wants or needs may conflict. Women, most often on the lower levels of the hierarchy, are in the position of the actual hands-on act of caring.

> Women are expected to care about and give care to others. But because of their lack of control over the caring process in many contexts, women's responsibility for caring remains ambiguous. In the home, women often lack such control because they lack the resources for caring. In human service bureaucracies, women lack control because they occupy lower-level positions. The constraints of professionalization often limit caregivers' attention to a narrow sphere, so that it becomes difficult for them to approach a situation "holistically." If they attempt to widen the sphere of their attention and to take more responsibility, they are often told they have "gone too far." If they stay within institutional limitations, their care-giving often seems inadequate to themselves and others. Care-receivers frequently blame them for not taking enough responsibility. (Fisher & Tronto, 1990, p. 44)

As Fisher and Tronto (1990) clearly stated, bureaucracy limits the ways in which caring can be exercised. If we create an ethic of caring in a school that continues to operate within a bureaucracy, will the limits of caring be extended? Will the resources—time, money, materials—be available to allow for reciprocal relationships, that is, for administrators and teachers to care for each other and students in ways they need and desire?

The ideal situation is for the care-giver to meet the needs of the care-receiver. The definition of "needs," however, is not easily established, particularly as power relations are unavoidable. As differences in power increase, there is a greater possibility for the dominant interests and ideas to take precedence in shaping the needs. For example, a local board of education may see low morale in a school in terms of aging teachers and poor children, rather than insufficient textbooks and other curricular materials. Or a principal may interpret the faculty's demands for budget information as a need for more power, rather than a need to feel trusted. Disconnection rather than caring occurs, and focus on the tensions between the care-giver and care-receiver usurps the attention from the complexity of caring.

No matter how close we come, the situation will never be "ideal." "Recognizing there will always be conflicts between human beings' needs and desires, our time may better be spent identifying and eliminating the most damaging and destructive forms of conflict" (Grimshaw, 1986, p. 186).

IMPLICATIONS: A POLITICS OF CARE

To strive to transform schools into places where people care is to reach for an ideal. Doing so is not simply to choose different methods of school organization and leadership, but it is to attempt to change a value system and system of moral reasoning traditional to citizens of the United States. Educational reformers seeking to transform schools where caring is nurtured, present a challenge to the moral fiber of the larger society. They suggest that connection be as valued as independence, that community be as important as autonomy, that moral reasoning be based on the contextual and particular rather than on universalizable principles, and that "difference" not be considered "deviance."

Feminist theory casts an ethic of caring as moral reasoning. As caring becomes a basis for school reform, it also becomes a politics of caring, centering on the dichotomy of female/male, private/public, and, in essence, care/power. As a politics of caring, it challenges males to integrate caring into their public as well as private lives; it necessitates a collective effort to implement and support caring; and it posits a balance of community with individualism, connection with autonomy, and interdependence with independence. An ethic of caring contests the notion of bureaucratic hierarchy as the best model on which to base organizational and leadership theory and practice.

There are several concerns, however, associated with school organization and leadership conceived within a framework of caring. Of primary importance is the relatively little attention given to interpreting caring as a collective effort. More difficult than determining another individual's best interests, ascertaining what is best for a group would seem to require the wisdom of Solomon. In schools or other institutions where bureaucracy has been the organization of choice and where hierarchy is assumed, persons living an ethic of caring would seek to balance top-down authority and decision-making with collaboration and shared decision-making. The questions become, how do people learn to collaborate, to come to agreement as a group, to agree to compromise on given individual interests so the group may flourish? How do people know when their personal interests outweigh those of the group?

Other concerns emanate from the notion of an ethic of caring as female. "Female," in general, is less valued in the public domain than "male." The characteristics of females and males, consequently, result in dichotomies that are judged by the gender with which they are associated; male qualities are of more value, female of lesser value. With that as the "given," working within an ethic of caring, rather than from a structure of bureaucracy, in the public domain will require a different way of thinking about male and female. It also will necessitate efforts to consider qualities associated with gender in gender-neutral ways and on a continuum, rather than as stark polarities. An ethic of caring needs to become gender-neutral.

As school reformers, and feminists among them, consider the need to make schools caring places, it is imperative that an ethic of caring be seen within the framework of the power structure already in place. An ethic of caring, pristine when viewed in a vacuum, is not without difficulties when implemented by human beings against a template of competition, individualism, and independence.

CHAPTER 3

The Story of Division High

People are always shouting they want to create a better future. It's not true. The future is an apathetic void of no interest to anyone. The past is full of life, eager to irritate us, provoke and insult us, tempt us to destroy or repaint it. The only reason people want to be masters of the future is to change the past. They are fighting for access to the laboratories where photographs are retouched and biographies and histories rewritten.
—Milan Kundera, *The Book of Laughter and Forgetting*, 1978

Understanding the history of Division High School (DHS) is critical to an understanding of the ways in which the staff initiated, developed, and perceived changes. Teachers and administrators, in the midst of current educational reforms, progressed insofar as they could address the past. They fought lingering pain from the memories of desegregation, from memories of too many failed reforms, from continuously adversarial relationships between teachers and administrators, and from events burned into their lives in the early years at Division. In terms of feminist standpoint theory, research is situated in locale and in personal identity. Thus, it is within the locale of Newtown that we begin to view the persons of the staff and students who determined the collective identity of Division High which, in turn, contributed to the identity of the unique individuals who constituted the high school.

IMPRESSIONS OF DIVISION HIGH

To me, Division High looked much like any other suburban school—a long, low, one-story brick building; athletic complex to one side; student parking lots sporting shiny, new cars; a faculty parking lot in the rear; and a signboard in front alerting passersby to the next home game, parent–teacher conference, or holiday. Flower boxes at the front of the school added color and a touch of softness to the otherwise institutional-looking building.

The school sat across the street from a well-kept neighborhood of modest houses, lawns, and gardens, and next to the city's only Catholic high school. A few blocks to the west were newer subdivisions and farmland. To the east, where many of the students lived, were poorly maintained houses surrounded by broken asphalt and dismantled vehicles.

My initial impressions of the school changed as I neared the building. Only one set of double doors was open, although there were at least four doors within my view. Heavy chains hung from them, securing all but the one. Security guards with walkie-talkies in hand patrolled the hallways and monitored the exits. Students, all staff members, and any person in Division on a regular basis wore an identification badge, which included her or his picture and status in the school.

Inside the building, floor-to-ceiling windows lighted the halls along the outer edges of the building. The hallways were clean and devoid of litter, despite the radical cuts in custodial work hours. And, to my surprise, the girls' bathrooms were not only clean, but had little, if any, graffiti. Virtually no classroom had windows; they were purposely designed that way to save money on fuel. The walls were half tile and half cinder block; the color, institutional drab. Classrooms were particularly colorless, as none had much in the way of materials. Books, maps, and equipment were not immediately apparent in any room. What materials there were, were locked up.

The library was beautiful, light, airy, and well used. The cafeteria was large with floor-to-ceiling windows on one side. There were a gym, swimming pool, and auditorium, as well as special classrooms designed for vocational education courses such as drafting. There were several rooms with computers for beginning computer instruction and use in business classes. Special education, as is typical of many schools, was located in the back of the school in several small rooms.

Students passed through the halls between classes with typical student exuberance; security guards, administrators, and teachers monitored the halls at those times. During classes, security guards patrolled the halls, checking students for ID badges and hall passes.

YESTERDAY

Recalling Division's opening in 1964, a counselor, there at the time and still a part of the staff, described the school as the "country club" of the Newtown School District. Innovative educational concepts influenced the architecture; the school had an abundance of amenities such as a swimming pool, auditorium, drivers' education track, and state-of-the-art athletic facilities. It attracted administrators and teachers who were interested in being "on the cutting edge." Located at the northernmost edge of the city, Division was adjacent to newly developed residential areas populated by economically and socially rising white, middle-class families. The school itself was not within the city limits. Because of the tremendous growth in housing developments in the north and because the residents of those developments wanted the school to be a part of the city system, the city council granted the Newtown Board of Education a variance to incorporate the school site into the city. All property surrounding the school site, including the parochial school next door, remained solely a part of the township.

There were 2,300 students in grades 10–12. Like the surrounding community, the student body was virtually white and middle or upper middle class; about 3% of the students were black and 1% Hispanic. The city celebrated Division's opening. School scrapbooks from 1964–1968 contain a myriad of newspaper clippings featuring Division students and teachers for academic and athletic accomplishments, or for their involvement in innovative school or classroom projects.

When Division opened, Newtown itself was experiencing growth and prosperity due to a flourishing and expanding industrial climate. It was a factory town, the majority of its populace employed in some capacity by the big industrial firms. As demand for their manufactured products increased, the firms continued to expand. People, including many African Americans from the South, flocked to the city, for working conditions, salaries, and benefits in the industrial plants far exceeded those in other blue-collar jobs. Workers credited those benefits to the intensity and success of the labor unions nationally and in Newtown specifically.

Newtown was a union town. The labor union took care of its people and they, in turn, had great allegiance to it. Likewise, the school district had a strong union, patterned after the city's labor unions. Strikes were common, but they produced results for the workers and teachers—benefits in working conditions and increased wealth. The union also produced what some people have described as a "union mentality." A Division teacher, born and reared in Newtown, whose father, brother, other relatives, and several friends work in factories, reflected on that perspective.

She described the attitude of Newtownians as one of the factory "owing" them a living and, more precisely, a more-than-comfortable life-style. The general line worker felt little personal responsibility for job satisfaction and job advancement. That stance, in turn, led to an attitude between management and labor that was adversarial and based on winning, not on compromise. The workers believed strikes were a natural and necessary part of life, and that there was no way to better working conditions or their lives without a bitter struggle against management. Workers' distrust of management was the norm; in fact, it was the expectation. That they worked for different and conflicting ends was assumed.

Because of the unions' success—labor and teachers'—Division High opened in a community that saw only continued prosperity and increasing wealth for all of Newtown's citizens. A member of the initial Division faculty recalls her first 3 years in the school.

> The morale was high; staff relationships were great both in and out of school. We had high parent involvement, probably because most of the parents were upper middle class and professionals. There were very few minority students, and those that were, were treated badly. [The principal] ran the show; it was his ship. He gave the teachers responsibility, but the ideas were his and we usually agreed with him. But he did give us responsibility. . . . [Division] was really seen as the "country club" of the [Newtown] schools. Teachers wanted to be here and parents wanted their kids here.

Within 4 years, the climate at Division began to change. The construction of an interstate through Newtown's downtown area displaced many black families. They subsequently moved to the north end of the city into dwellings constructed by the U.S. Department of Housing and Urban Development (HUD). Ironically, the north end had been a "red line area" for blacks. That is, whites would not sell houses in that region to blacks, thus maintaining all-white neighborhoods and schools. With the construction of the HUD housing and the almost simultaneous federal mandates for desegregation of schools, there was a significant increase in enrollment of black students at DHS.

> The freeways were starting to come through [Newtown] in '67—well they were starting to buy the land for [the interstate]. . . . So a lot of the neighborhoods, which you call ghetto neighborhoods, down by [the plant], where it's not worth much, those families were displaced, at a pretty good price for their homes. And they moved out to other areas. And the only area that they could buy homes in was the [Division] area. And then, of course, blockbusting started. Do you know what blockbusting is? [No.] When the state kind of goes into a . . . house in a white district, and offers the people a fantastic price for a house, and gets a black person in there. Then they go to the other people up and down the block, and they say, "Hey, you know, there's blacks moving in down the block. You better sell and sell in a hurry."

The influx of African Americans into the north end initiated the beginnings of "white flight." The newly developed white, middle-class community suddenly became a largely black community as the former owners left their new homes to flee from—as one teacher commented—"those niggers." A teacher recalled his having bought a new home across from the school. When black families began buying into the neighborhood, "with the blessing of the Johnson administration," a white neighbor packed his family into the car, locked the door of the house, and never returned, not even to sell the house.

By 1968–69, the percentage of African Americans at Division had increased dramatically to 30%, according to a faculty member. Racial tensions began to build. A current DHS staff member who taught in another Newtown high school in the late 1960s and early 1970s recalled his memories of that period at Division and elsewhere in the district.

> In '68, '69, '70, I want to tell you that [Division] was an armed philo-sophical camp divided into two warring factions. I'm telling you it was ugly. It was ugly. I mean to the point where they had police cars screeching to a halt on the lawn with their sirens on, kids beating each other up, extortion in the bathrooms, faculty confrontations, threats against teachers, kids ganging up, beating up—not beating up—but it got to the point where the football coach left because he was threat-ened by his own football players. . . . At [my school] we had a group of kids that threatened to shoot the administrators who came in the build-ing. We had the police over on the railroad tracks to stop snipers who were slated to be in the railroad tracks over at [my school]. I'm telling . . . we've gone through some really tough times. [There was] a princi-pal [at Division] that was trying to bend over backwards. You've got to understand the timing of this. Martin Luther King had just been killed. Bobby Kennedy had just been killed. There were the '67 De-troit riots, and God, there was the animosity and the stress, and the ra-cial tension was the proverbial "so thick you could cut it with a knife." I mean it was really ugly.

On April 4, 1968, according to another teacher at DHS, "all hell broke loose when Dr. King was assassinated. For 2 years it was an unmitigated nightmare." Many current faculty members could recall that police were inside and outside the building, and they used tear gas to break up fights. There were students fighting students, teachers fighting teachers, students and teachers fighting. A teacher was suspended for using a racial epithet against a student. The staff was split along racial lines and along liberal/conservative lines. The teachers recalled incidents where faculty members had fistfights in the halls, and to avoid fights the principal banned certain teachers from using the lounge at the same time. When the police finally left the building, parents volunteered to patrol the halls. According to one teacher, there was "total disharmony" for 2 or 3 years. "Nobody wanted to come here—staff or kids. [long pause] And we've never recovered."

Despite the fact that all Newtown's schools suffered from racial tensions and riots, the perception of the teachers and the community members is that

Division had the most difficulty. Several Division teachers believed that the media consistently used the school to illustrate the problems stemming from desegregation, and have all but concluded that the media was responsible for DHS's plummet from "country club school" to district pariah.

An African American teacher, who entered DHS in 1972 as a ninth-grade student, vividly recalled her high school years. Hurt and anger permeated her voice and her face as she recounted her struggles with the school's poor reputation in the aftermath of the race riots. Her pain was obvious as she remembered the energy necessary to regain the high academic standards that DHS surrendered when it became a primarily "black" school.

> I can remember being a student here and we were protesting because they were reducing college prep classes and creating more general ed classes. . . . But I think in '72 I felt branded. . . . And then I would say that I fought uphill battles for the rest of my time here to prove that this was not a bad school. You know, that we received an adequate education. So, whenever we were in some kind of competition for the school, you had to know what you were talking about and then all of those kinds of your behavior had to be really on target.

Corroborating this former Division student's perceptions of the school's reputation and struggle for higher-level academic preparation are the reflections of a science teacher who transferred to DHS shortly after desegregation. As background, it is useful to know that the Newtown community elected to use magnet classes as their method of desegregation. Through a combination of choice and assignment, each high school focused on particular academic magnet classes; additionally, each also had specific vocational emphases. Division's magnet classes were to revolve around computers and technology. However, because of limited equipment and public relations, that was not successful.

The school also was to be a science and math magnet, despite the fact that the high school closest to it already was known for its expertise in those discipines. The irony is not that there were two schools with the same magnet, but that

> [Division's] science and math magnet program in the early '70s was a second thought [for] the creators of the magnet program because that meant the black students would have to go where there were white students to get science and math. So they decided to put one here.

The magnet program was developed to implement desegregation, but it served to keep black students at DHS, a predominantly black school. It also resulted in a curtailment of the original science and math magnet classes at another Newtown high school. Funding was lower for DHS's program, for the school could not attract students from other schools because of the transportation scheduling.

> [The] transportation scheduling . . . does not give you a chance for the [other high school] students to come here. Well, they could come . . . but would go to [the other school] because of the fact that it was the same distance and they started earlier. The fact that we start third in the sequence of schools, that once you come over here, I mean you've lost an hour just going back to school.

Additionally, DHS's science and math magnet program did not begin until the second year of the district magnet program, and thus it fell behind the already established science and math classes at the other high school. At the time of this study, DHS continued to struggle with its science program. There were earth science and biology classes, and only one small chemistry class. There were no advanced chemistry or physics classes.

From another perspective, DHS teachers viewed the district magnet program as hurting the quality of academics offered at the school because any significantly above-average student was encouraged to take academic classes at other schools. Faculty members felt deprived of working with the higher-quality students. In fact, there were few advanced classes offered in any academic subject area.

> I always felt bad . . . that our counselors were willing to send students to take upper-level science and math at [the other school]. And they did it as a favor to the students. And, therefore, we did not have good, our own good students to enroll in our classes, let alone trying to entice students from other schools to come over here.

Because of the rioting and fighting reported at Division in the late 1960s and early 1970s, the school gained the reputation of being the roughest, toughest school in the area. Teachers, by and large, did not choose to go there because the academic program was weak. The perception among the staff was that DHS had a disproportionate number of students who had trouble academically. Many parents believed the school's reputation: rough, tough, and academically inferior. They did not want to send their children there and did anything they could to enroll them in another high school, even sending them to private schools. Division, once seen as the premier school, became the school for "misfits."

> One of the problems, the big problems, for our school has been the magnet program. I see that the program screened out even our normal

share of bright kids in the district. Kids that belong in our neighborhood school district . . . go to other schools. And the magnet program allowed them to do that. However, the reason they go to other schools is that their parents know of our undeserved reputation. . . . Many parents will do anything to keep their kid from going here. . . . Give a different address . . . to go to another school. Change kids' custody, you know, give the custody of the kid to an uncle who lives in [another school's] district. . . . I think we have a disproportionate number of kids who are in trouble academically. And they don't have the benefit of seeing as many of the bright school chums as they might, you know, in a positive academic world.

After the events of desegregation and the resultant downward adjustment of the academic program, DHS continued to struggle, fighting an uphill battle to regain its positive reputation. The first black principal, who was appointed in the aftermath of the efforts toward integration, was, according to a former counselor, "a disgrace, a thief. He was dishonorable toward women." He was removed from the school because of embezzling funds that parents had collected for new band uniforms; he was never formally charged and was moved "up" to the district office. During the time he was at Division, the assistant football coach, who was black, was accused of sexual involvement with cheerleaders and subsequently was dismissed.

Unspoken and formally denied inferences to the problems at DHS as the result of black leadership abounded among the white teachers and community members. Racial tension—unacknowledged and denied—hovered in the air and served to maintain or increase the split among faculty, which had begun during the movement to desegregate. The attitude of the faculty, as well as community members, toward new teachers was, "What did you do to get on some principal's shit list?" Needless to say, the morale of faculty and staff was, according to an older teacher, "low and sinking."

The next principal was no newcomer to DHS, having served as deputy principal under the school's first chief administrator. However, he came from the rival high school, bringing an entourage of teachers with him, which was generally not unexpected. A problem arose, however, when he replaced all the department chairpersons with "his" people. The staff, already greatly split, became even more divided.

When he left, another black male became principal. Generally, the faculty saw him as a sincere person who was good with students. However, he was educationally ineffective and passive, having virtually no innovative curriculum ideas and evidencing little energetic response to educational initiatives. Above all, he had "no clout" with "downtown." The staff viewed themselves as leaderless.

As the second black principal who seemed to accomplish little, he was particularly berated by white, male teachers, especially those who had administrative aspirations and continually were passed over. Racial biases were denied by most faculty members. Teachers coming to DHS continued to be viewed as casualties of another principal's dissatisfaction with them. The splits among staff increased and deepened; mutual wariness and distrust grew; and the problems at the core—racial bias and tension, distrust—remained silenced. That principal had the longest tenure, 13 years, of any administrator at DHS. No major incidences, positive or negative, occurred in the high school during that time. Discontent, throughout the school and throughout the community, continued to fester and grow.

TODAY

At the time of this study, the student body of Division was 98% African American, and headed by a black, female principal, the first *female* high school principal in Newtown's history. About 50% of the teachers were African American and 50% were white. The prevalent description of DHS was that of a school on the brink of collapse. Two teachers described it as "a beautiful new house with a carefully manicured lawn, *but* the family within is falling apart," and as "a house of cards that's going to come tumbling down."

Division High suffered from the effects of the city's dramatic decline. Unlike 30 years earlier, the city was no longer thriving, but was fighting for survival. The once active and expanding industrial plants were closed. Formerly prosperous and upwardly mobile families were without jobs or worked in situations providing only subsistence living. Families left the city, many returning to the South. The decrease in school population was striking. Within 3 years, Division's student body dropped from over 2,000 to less than 1,600. As a result, classes became larger and materials fewer.

Students and teachers lived with the rumors that Division would be closed if the district continued to lose students. Both groups understood that DHS was the most expendable of the high schools in the district. Because of the rumors, teachers believed their budget was less than those of other district high schools; the support, generally, from the district *was* less.

At the same time as the staff lived with the threat of the school closing, the board of education and the superintendent provided opportunities for school and curricular reforms. Site-based management (SBM), shared decision-making, and alliances with the local business community and a local university were some of the opportunities presented to the staff. However, they did not come without difficulties.

The threat of closing affected the attitude of the staff toward making substantial changes. People either supported change, hoping to keep Division open, or refused to waste effort on innovations because they believed the school would close anyway. The latter feeling was intensified by the belief that Division's district had little, if any, political power. Those attitudes had a significant effect on the attempt to establish SBM and shared decision-making as methods of school organization and leadership.

> It's very difficult to make change. And I think most people feel that if a school is closed it's going to be [Division]. . . . I think there's a perception that why bother because it's [SBM] not going to make a difference anyway, and I think the other side of that is some people feel we have to make this work because it's the only hope we have of not being closed. That if we can, if we can do something that is so successful, and we can show that it's successful, then [the board of education] is going to have to look at closing somebody else. . . . I feel that we have to do something that is so successful, that it will make it very difficult to close [Division] because I don't think this community has the political clout to keep it open. The other communities all have more political clout.

Perhaps even more important to the establishment of SBM at Division was the influence of the teachers' union. Like the labor unions in Newtown, the teachers' union in its early years was very strong, negotiating for teachers *against* administrators, and maintaining the adversarial relationship. The union members were willing to strike in order to attain their goals. A DHS teacher, who was actively involved in the union for almost 30 years, implied that the attitude of its members was even more antagonistic toward administration than were labor unions: "I've been on seven strikes as a teacher, which is more than any [labor union] member who's my age has participated in."

In recent years, however, the union lost some of its power, and some teachers believed its role needed to be redefined. The membership was no longer fully supportive of union activities, resulting in a split between those who were union supporters and those who were not. Those attitudes contributed to the difficulties experienced in the development of SBM at Division High.

There seemed to be general agreement that the union played an integral part in having site-based management piloted in some of the Newtown schools. The agreement ended there. For nonunion supporters, SBM was union-conceived and union-driven. They saw the union as using SBM to grasp—or regain—power within the district by putting teachers in a position to make and carry out school policy. Some even felt that the union "convinced" DHS administrators, who initially voted against SBM, to change their minds—and their votes. For those reasons, the nonunionists particularly dragged their feet regarding the implementation of SBM or actively rebelled against it.

Union members, however, believed that SBM was the last chance for DHS—and the entire Newtown school district—to survive educationally, and the union had the strength to ensure its acceptance by administration; they did not view SBM as a way for the union to gain power. Rather, they saw the union as an integral part of saving the educational system generally and Division High in particular. Faculty members on the initial SBM steering committee were all strong unionists, active at city, regional, and state levels. The principal felt a strong unionist attitude from that initial committee, "an orientation of them against us," which immediately caused tension between faculty and administration, and limited collaboration.

Teachers believed that the media continued to slight or ignore Division's accomplishments and emphasize the school's problems. State honors in a science and engineering competition were not recognized by the city's newspaper or local television station. Crimes and assaults by students routinely were in print and on the air. A secretary whose child attended DHS commented:

> I know that [DHS] could not have the best of reputations, but I don't feel that we probably have any more problems than any other school has. Ours are always spread out, and everybody knows when [DHS] has a problem.

Division seemed to be fighting a losing battle because of its history and negative reputation. Teachers rarely came to the school voluntarily; they most often transferred involuntarily from another school to fill needed positions, or chose DHS as the lesser of two evils in terms of the better course assignment. Division's reputation weighed heavily on teachers.

> If [DHS] was seen to be a premier school like [another Newtown school], you wouldn't have staff members feeling this way. . . . They've always operated under a cloud. . . . People treat you like a hero because you've made it through another year. You know, you're a Rambo or something.

Parents continued to find ways to send their children to other schools in or out of the district. And Division continued to receive students no other school wanted.

> We are a dumping ground. We have blue slip kids in here all the time; they [administrators] don't bother to tell you they're blue slips. Those are the kids that are kicked out of another high school and told never

to come back and then we have to pick them up. And under the code of conduct, a person who has been kicked out of one of the high schools . . . and put in another [high] school is there on probation, and if probation is broken, simply by getting in trouble again, that's a rule that's never followed. . . . We have kids in the classroom now that are awaiting trial for felonies. . . . We didn't know he had an ankle tether on until his trial came up and then he's gone. What are the teachers' reaction to these goings on? "The number one rule is cover your ass, the rest is bullshit."

And as another teacher summed up, "I guess if we look at the history of [Division], it's always been a school for misfits, so to speak."

With this history, Division High School—a school in a once thriving city now struggling to survive, a school with many divisions—embarked on making changes. Could its constituents pursue an ethic of caring in a school that historically had been fraught with power struggles for control? Or would that prove impossible or personally too costly?

CHAPTER 4

The Principal: Care-Giver

There is nothing more difficult to take in hand, more perilous of conduct, or more uncertain in its success, than to take the lead in the introduction of a new order of things.
— N. Machiavelli, *The Prince*

As I thought about Mattie Johnson, I envisioned her leading faculty, staff, students, and the neighborhood community into a new era for Division High. She had prepared herself for years to be the principal—the leader—of a school. Finally, she was in that position. Her leadership, however, was vastly different from what she had anticipated, for expectations were that she would introduce "a new order of things." She viewed that new order as recreating Division as a caring place. She did not foresee, however, the degree of change needed in order to establish a climate in which caring could grow and thrive.

Current school reform efforts, to varying degrees, focus on community–school partnerships (Goodlad, 1988, 1990; Holmes Group, 1986, 1988; Sizer, 1985, 1992). The thrust of those partnerships is to balance authority and control of schools through decision-making and management that are shared among teachers, administrators, students, parents, and other community members. The alliances aim to develop schools that are more people-centered, relational, and collaborative in their functioning, that is, places where people care for one another. The intention, in essence, is in sync with feminist notions of alternatives to bureaucracy and hierarchy: to develop organizations that are grounded in an ethic of caring.

School organizational patterns founded on a hierarchy of leadership are counterproductive to caring. A community–school partnership requires the recognition and acceptance of multiple beliefs, values, and viewpoints among the members of the organization. Conceding that there will be differences among them, and working toward the welfare not only of the individual but also of the group, members need to experience trust and a willingness to be *inter*dependent. In other words, the institutional structure needs to change to accommodate diversity among its constituents. Hierarchical organization does not support interdependence, which is necessary for cooperation; thus, institutional structure demands modification to accommodate personalities as they attempt to work individually *and* collectively. Such a climate and organizational structure, ultimately, sustain and nurture caring among members.

To establish schools based on an ethic of caring would not be a simple task. Power relations drive current organizational structure. School leaders attempting to nurture caring must recognize that it will be embedded within the power structure of a bureaucratic hierarchy. Consequently, if schools are to be caring places, the relationship between caring and power must be considered. Power relationships exist. An ethic of caring as the basis for organizational structure and culture, realistically, will coexist with power, therefore necessitating an exploration of what that relationship will or can be.

In the process of effecting such changes, the concept of leadership needs to be re-examined and the role of "leader," perhaps, redefined. In a community-oriented organizational structure, the intention is for teachers, students, parents, and community members to assume aspects of leadership by taking part in critical decisions affecting the school, the curriculum, and the students. In essence, the leadership role may be distributed among many.

With such changes in organizational structure, it will be incumbent on principals to consider their roles, not only in the final analysis, but in the change process itself. There appears to be no model for them to follow as their positions shift from that of primary decision-maker and building authority, to one sharing decision-making and management with people from within and, possibly, from outside the school. Leadership could be shared and shifted, at varying times, among teachers, students, parents, and other community members, in addition to building administrators. In the process of moving from the concept of one leader—the principal—to that of shared leadership, there is the assumption that the principal's changed role will evolve or, as some may speculate, devolve. In either case, the principal's role in the *process* of change deserves thoughtful consideration. The way the role is viewed during that period may affect not only the implementation of reform strategies, but also the conceptions and subsequent definitions of "leadership" and of "caring."

In this chapter, I explore the ways in which Mattie Johnson, principal, intentionally and unintentionally dealt with the role of care-giver, which she gave herself, and the role of leader/authority, which was both assigned to and willingly accepted by her. Through her experiences, we begin to see caring and power in relationships that appear symbiotic or, perhaps, parasitic. Regardless of the labeling, the reality becomes one of connection, not dichotomy, between caring and power.

As principal, Mattie viewed herself as being about "the business of really caring about people, really, truly, knowing everybody is important." She believed in "the respecting, the dignity, the worth of every individual . . . nurturing, caring, and understanding." Although she did not associate herself with feminism, her description of how she wanted to lead and be perceived as a leader were very much within the realm of feminist theorists' exploration of organization and leadership emanating from an ethic of care. Her intent was to effect an atmosphere of caring in Division High School—indeed, a new order of things.

Several pertinent questions surfaced in my deliberation of the principal's function in the process of change: (1) How did she understand, interpret, and enact caring? (2) Did she see herself as the primary care-giver? (3) Did she envision herself as a recipient of caring from faculty, staff, and/or students? (4) How did she promote caring among the staff and between students and staff? (5) How did she understand, interpret, and enact power? (6) Did she believe she needed power in order to enact caring? (7) Would her evolving role affect organizational change that supported an ethic of caring?

The story of Mattie Johnson addresses those questions. Through her experiences and reflections, we become intimately involved in her attempts to make a transition between the known—traditional concepts of leadership as authority and control—and the unknown—an amorphous vision of shared leadership—and in her attempts to move toward an ethic of caring while immersed in a structure of "power over."

MATTIE JOHNSON—BACKGROUND OF A PRINCIPAL

> People who really know me, know that I, for the most part, am very nurturing and caring and understanding. I am a people person. I really love people. I am really concerned about people.

Mattie Johnson worked her way into a principalship. As one DHS staff member put it, she came up through the ranks, paying her dues to the system and working for everything she had ever achieved.

Although she spent her early years in the South, virtually her entire educational career was in Newtown. She began as a social studies teacher, advancing to department chair, assistant principal, and, then, deputy principal, the position just below that of principal. During Mattie's years as a lower-level administrator, the head of the school was her mentor, grooming her to become a high school principal.

When Mattie was deputy principal at another school, financial cutbacks in the district forced teacher and administrator layoffs, and she was "pink-slipped." Just weeks prior to the new school year, she received notification of her reinstatement into her school; the position, however, was not the same. An administrator from another school and with more seniority took Mattie's position, reducing her to assistant principal.

Although pleased to have a position in the same school, Mattie did not find the return easy. Being demoted meant that she might very possibly have to wait even longer to have her own building. She had conflicting feelings about being replaced by a white male on the verge of retirement whom, because of her commitment to the school, she felt obligated to mentor in the traditions and information of her school. She was hurt and angry, but determined not to begin the school year with such feelings but to make the most of a disappointing and frustrating situation.

As was typical of Mattie, she picked herself up, believing there was a purpose for her setback. After all, she had recovered from temporary blindness as a child and learned to compensate for her poor vision.[5] She continued to pursue her goal of becoming a secondary school principal, believing she would achieve it if she worked diligently. There were no excuses for her not to achieve.

> My upbringing, my father, my mother insisted that anything you do, you do well . . . every tub has to stand on its own bottom. That you don't expect other people to do your work for you. Blind or not, woman or not, poor or not, black or not, you just don't do that. I learned those things very well.

She returned to school that fall as assistant principal, determined to do her best. Her sensitivity, warmth, and understanding permeated the school. In my role as a research assistant that year, I heard from teachers, unsolicited and time and again, that Mrs. Johnson was a very caring person; that she could be tough, but she was fair; that they could argue with her, but always felt that she said her piece and did not hold a grudge; that she was always honest with them and they knew where she stood on any issue.

The following year she was offered the position of deputy principal at Division High School, a step closer to becoming principal of her own building. Her reputation followed her. At Division, teachers describing her cited explicitly her strength, her fairness, and her charisma. An original staff member of Division summed up the new deputy as "a good person. . . . She is an educator . . . she's very rigid, very firm, but very fair . . . *she cares*, she cares, she cares!"

Mattie used that year to learn about the school, to get to know the teachers and students, and to effect a few changes. She worked especially hard to understand the culture and community, the nuances that made DHS unique, and the features that made it a pariah among the city's high schools. When she was appointed to the principalship in July 1991, she had a sense of the students, teachers, and other staff members; the breadth and depth of the problems faced by the school; her general expectations of herself as a leader; and her general goals for the school.

With those thoughts in mind, she set five goals for herself: (1) to improve academic achievement and promote excellence in education; (2) to build trust among staff and administrators, and among staff and students; (3) to extend site-based management and shared decision-making to include a wider variety of people, especially parents, in the management of the school; (4) to improve communications between and among staff and the total community; and (5) to improve school–community relations.

Within the first months of Mattie's principalship, she was feted throughout the community and school district. She was the first female high school principal in Newtown's history—and she was African American. Members of social organizations, friends and relatives, and the school district staff all celebrated her promotion. The community, the district, and the staff at Division High all looked to her as the *one* who would change Division. Hopes, expectations, and spirits were at a new high. Additionally, women, particularly black women, were enormously proud to have a sister who had persevered and won.

But what did she win? She acquired a school with a faculty who wanted, yet resisted, leadership; who wanted to be cared for, but were accustomed to controlling. She acquired "partnerships" with community organizations and a local university, both of which wanted to help DHS, but on their own terms and for their own purposes. She acquired a position of authority, the principal-ship, but with a mandate to alter the organizational structure to accommodate *shared* decision-making and *shared* management. She wanted to believe her position was one of leadership and power, one that she would temper with caring. But the ambiguity of her position and her power—what she thought they should be and what they were in reality—was quick to surface.

Mattie entered the school year "on a honeymoon," as she liked to say. Bouquets adorned her office on a regular basis; notes of congratulations arrived daily; several articles about her, including a feature story, were in the city newspaper; and parents, community members, businesspersons, and others dropped in to wish her well. But no one really told her what was expected of her. They just knew *she* would make a difference. They were counting on her.

MATTIE JOHNSON—CARE-GIVER

And she did make a difference. With Mattie Johnson's arrival as principal, the air at Division High was charged with expectations and a readiness, of sorts, for change. Faculty, staff, and community members looked forward to Mattie's coming, for she brought with her a reputation of caring, concern, and a sense of quality and pride for the school and all those associated with it. She was a breath of fresh air in a school that stagnated with painful histories; she was a symbol of change in a building where people and ideas languished. Those characteristics, although not explicitly articulated, permeated the staff's illusions of the transformations that could take place.

In the following sections, I discuss the ways in which Mattie intended to develop caring at Division. She believed that by modeling caring; by establishing pride in and within Division; by building trust; by having high expectations for self, staff, and students; by accepting her own and other's humanity; by "ministering" to faculty and students; and by building community, she could establish an atmosphere in which faculty, staff, and students would learn to give and receive caring.

Building Pride in Division

> Your leader will set the tone. People pick up on the habits of their leaders and I have found that to be true.

Mattie Johnson wanted to set a new tone, one of caring, for DHS. She recognized that the accumulation of years of hurt, pain, and distrust among the faculty and staff would not dissipate overnight. She therefore determined to care for individuals and the school community as a whole in ways that demanded little of them in return. Her aim was to provide opportunities for them to gain the needed strength to recreate respect and concern for, and trust in, one another. For Mattie, setting the tone strongly indicated leadership based on her serving the community.

She began by altering the building physically to portray beauty, light, warmth, and joy to all who had contact with DHS. Ultimately, her hope was to create an atmosphere in which faculty, staff, students, and residents of the local neighborhood would rebuild trust and respect for one another. She also hoped that the entire community would embrace the school as an integral part of their lives.

The first projects were remodeling and refurnishing the deputy principal's and principal's offices, removing a wall separating a secretary from the others, refurnishing the faculty lounge, putting flowers and plants in the main office, making the floor-to-ceiling windows at the front of the building a virtual greenhouse with a variety of hanging and stationary plants, and installing a soup, sandwich, and salad bar in the faculty dining room so staff would not have to go through the students' lunch line. She insisted that students respect the building by keeping it clean. Whenever she saw litter in the hallways, she would either pick it up herself or ask a student to remove it. Discipline for students included students scrubbing graffiti from the walls. Mattie believed that one's physical surroundings contributed to the feeling that one had not only about the place but, more important, about one's place in it. Her use of "one" included the community as a whole: parents, community members, and visitors, as well as faculty, students, and staff.

> *If* we are about the business of servicing students, serving community, what do I feel? What do you feel when you walk into the main office? . . . How do people treat you? What do you see when you first drive up to this campus? Is there a sense of business, but is it caring, is it friendly? Do you sense that people want to be here and you want to be here? I didn't feel that when I walked in [the main office]. Why are these windows up here? Why is the secretary enclosed away, and people told me that is the way it has been. What message does this send? . . . We can be the best school in the world, but in my opinion, how you look [is important]. . . . I also believe that before we get a chance to do our jobs in our classrooms, that people make a decision about who we are and what we are by walking into this building and these offices. . . . I do believe an orderly, clean, caring environment . . . helps with the mission. . . . I just didn't see that people would get the sense of feeling safe, cared for, [or feel that] "I am here to serve you."

Mattie intended the physical refurbishings to be a token of her commitment to the deeper, more significant organizational and curricular alterations that would "take time" to bring about. She saw this work, albeit "window dressing," as she called it, as a concrete way of showing the faculty she cared. Her dream was for faculty and students to be proud of themselves and the achievements they made. But she knew that the negative perception of the school, about and by its students and teachers, would not disappear because she wished it to. Changes necessary to alter those perceptions would take time. Therefore, she wanted to demonstrate tangibly and immediately to staff and students her pride in the school and her faith in them.

Building Trust

Building trust among the faculty and between the faculty and administration was of major importance to the new principal. Relationships within the school, by teachers' own admission, were fragmented and distrustful. The lack of trust between administrators and teachers stemmed from not only the history of the school, but also the history of the community.

As noted earlier, Newtown was a strong union town. Despite educators' primary affiliation in the 1960s and 1970s with the National Education Association, then known as the "nonunion" teacher organization, Newtown teachers patterned their association after the successful tactics based on adversarial relations between labor and management of the United Auto Workers of America.

An attitude of antagonism between teachers and administrators permeated the schools within the district. Given the difficulties of desegregation faced by DHS, and given its ensuing reputation as the "roughest" and "worst" school in the city, relations between administration and faculty escalated in their contentiousness. As much as faculty wanted to believe that Mattie would bring positive changes to the school, they did so with the underlying distrust honed on years of viewing administration as "the enemy."

Mattie knew that faculty needed to trust her, and she them. Soon after she became principal, she commented that "one of the things [we need] is the building of trust, and as you well know that takes time . . . it wears me out." The faculty would need time to observe her before they ventured their own tentative extensions of trust to her and to each other, and she would have to have the patience to let them. She thought carefully about her role in creating a climate of trust.

One way to build trust was to be visible and accessible to faculty and students. Early in the school year, Mattie seemed superhuman as she appeared almost magically throughout the building, hour by hour, day in and day out. She stood in the outer office in the mornings to banter with faculty members as they arrived. She joined teachers and staff in the hallways prior to the beginning of the school day and as students passed from class to class. She kept her office door open, inviting faculty and staff to visit with her at any time. She wandered through the student cafeteria during the various lunch hours to tease students or to ask them about themselves. She made a point of stopping by teachers' rooms, just to say "hi." She ambled into the kitchen to visit with the cooks and cafeteria aides. She seemed always present to compliment and thank volunteers who came and left the building on no certain schedule. To Mattie, her visible interest in the members of the school community signaled that she cared for and about them.

Most important to her was initiating personal contact with each teacher in order to establish communication, at least on a professional level, between teachers and administrators, as well as among teachers. To her, communication was a dialogue and an integral part of building trust, necessary for SBM and shared decision-making to be effective. Because of the controversy among the staff regarding the understanding and implementation of SBM (to be discussed later), and because of the history of antagonistic relationships between administration and staff, Mattie was convinced that administrators and teachers must talk with one another in ways that would develop and sustain positive working relationships. Through individual contacts with staff members, and by demonstrating her sincerity about working together as a team and, therefore, persuading them of her integrity and the need for such honesty throughout the school community, Mattie hoped to change the attitudes of administrators and teachers toward one another.

Her goal at the beginning of the year was to have had an individual conference with every teacher, and with groups of support staff, before the school year ended. She wanted to show her personal interest in, and to discuss her expectations of, the individual and/or group, and to encourage teachers and staff to voice their expectations of her as principal. She viewed herself as a model, one who listened, one who inquired, and one who shared. Trust grew as a result of people knowing one another; she wanted to know the teachers and wanted them to know her as their leader.

> The more I talk to [the teachers], the better they know me. The more I do what I say that I am going to do, and the more I get a chance to hear them out, the better job and the more trust will build.

Building trust meant building relationships; building relationships meant changing the ways staff had learned to interact over the years. She hoped that talking with staff one on one would open communication throughout the school community and prepare them to work as a team. She did not accept that she alone was responsible for "changing" Division High; change would be the result of team effort. Ever aware that change takes time, Mattie committed herself to building trust slowly and solidly, certain that patience and small, steady steps were more effective than flashy proposals or projects that dazzle like fireworks and fade as rapidly.

> Well, you deal with [changes] one at a time. . . . But some people thought that "[Mattie Johnson's] coming," . . . [Mattie Johnson] was going to fix it. But what I . . . said is . . . "Wait! Whoa! This is collaboration. This is team work. This is shared decision-making. This is shared responsibility." But that takes time. . . . That's why it's so important that time be spent building trust. I can't do that in a year. . . . I know that it takes time to build relationships. And that's what we're building.

Honesty and integrity were of utmost importance to Mattie, personally and professionally. From a professional standpoint, integrity was critical to her in building relationships founded on trust. Making an effort to talk with people was necessary, but the bottom line was that people trust her because she was honest and straightforward.

> It has always been important to me that people believe what I say. Integrity, I must have that. You may not like me, you may not agree with me . . . but the real compliment is when people say that [Mattie Johnson] cares about people and that if she tells you something . . . that is what she believes. That is a compliment.

Mattie was concerned particularly about the "anti-administration" attitude of some of the members of the steering committee, which, loosely, was the governing body of SBM. Most of the members had strong union ties. She indicated it was useless to think that they would automatically trust her because the school, ostensibly, was attempting site-based management and shared decision-making. "We've had three strong union people who have been accustomed [to seeing] the administration as the enemy and that you've got to have this tug of war." The "us-against-them" attitude among the unionists prevailed and would not be dissipated simply because the school was initiating SBM.

She perceived that she and the steering committee members had not *really* discussed her role or theirs in the framework of SBM; therefore, they were unsure and tentative about what to expect from each other. In order to build trust between herself and the committee members, she needed to work with them individually and within the group. Communication on many levels was necessary to establish the trust needed to begin the process of defining their roles and their mission. Only then might they be able to work together. And that would take time.

Despite her initial intentions, communication and building trust proved to be more difficult than she had imagined. About 6 weeks into the school year, Mattie twisted her ankle, requiring her to wear a removable cast and orthopedic shoes. That incident seemed to be a major turning point in the way she began to function and think about her role as leader. Although she continued, on a limited basis, to stand in the hallway outside her office between classes and to greet faculty each morning, she generally became less visible in the building. The accident limited her mobility, causing her to stay in her office for larger portions of the day. The more time she spent at her desk, the more Mattie seemed to feel she needed to be there, citing private conferences, phone calls, and paperwork as the compelling forces. By December, I noticed that her door rarely was open. Faculty complained about her inaccessibility, pointing to newly established office hours, which all but eliminated "dropping in" to chat for a few minutes about things of no particular import, and which relegated teachers to her "formal" schedule. Faculty also resented her being out of the building to attend district and regional school meetings.

Mattie appeared unaware of the changes she had made, for they seemed to have evolved more from unplanned circumstances than as a result of conscious decisions. At the end of the year, she reflected on the increased demands placed on her, which teachers perceived as limiting her visibility in the school and their immediate access to her. That presented a dilemma for Mattie: How did she understand what were realistic and unrealistic expectations of her in light of her own and faculty expectations, and what was simply stretching to reach her ideals?

She seemed to understand the faculty's frustration with her, but experienced discomfort in what she wanted from them. She implied that she wanted an interdependent, not a dependent, relationship with them, yet she continued to envision herself as "leader," the one in control. She wanted the teachers to understand that she needed their caring. Her interpretation was that they would not expect her to single-handedly transform the school and would recognize *their* need to collaborate to identify common goals for DHS. Despite knowing intellectually and emotionally that she alone could not physically and mentally accomplish all the changes needed and expected, Mattie, at the end of the school year, recognized that she had failed to communicate those thoughts to the teachers.

> [The teachers and administrators] were unrealistic; they saw me as being able to solve all of the problems. . . . [I believe] visibility is critical. But, visible in the sense of being supportive and not being hands-on. . . . I have to delegate; I can't survive if I can't do that. . . . The staff members became critical [of my not being in the halls and visiting classrooms]. You know, it was important to me, too. . . . I should have communicated that more to the staff. . . . I'm going to have to talk to them more and communicate the fact that it's a team effort. That they're burying me, they are literally burying me and I will become resentful because I will not be able to keep up that kind of pace.

Listening to her, I felt her bristle at the notion that the faculty thought they could control her, or that they seemed to think that she would be at their "beck and call." Mattie was not pleased with the faculty's failure to understand her obligations to be out of the building. As a new principal, and as the only female high school principal, she was particularly sensitive to the importance of being at meetings within the district or at regional administrative meetings. She saw her attendance as representing DHS in the upper levels of the bureaucracy and, therefore, enhancing Division's position in the district through opportunities presented her as the school leader. However, she did not—nor as the administrator did she feel the need to—tell the teachers her rationale for leaving them. Although establishing better communication among faculty was a step leading to trust, Mattie found that she had difficulty communicating her needs.

Being a leader, for Mattie, seemed to involve more than meeting faculty needs; it meant fulfilling her role in the bureaucracy. As she tried to meet bureaucratic expectations, she also attempted to weave them into her own visions for Division High.

Having High Expectations for Self, Staff, and Students

To Mattie, having high expectations for self, others, and students was synonymous with a school staff that cared for and about students. She believed that, as principal, she set the tone for everyone in the building; therefore, she expected as much, or more, of herself as she did from the staff. From her outward appearance to the minute details of a report, Mattie consistently attempted to model the best. Whatever she assumed of staff, she willingly did first—patrol or pick up debris in the halls, know students on a personal level, or show caring and understanding toward colleagues. She saw herself as highly organized and efficient, not wanting to settle for anything less than perfection.

> I have high expectations of myself and [of] people with whom I work.
> A leader sets the tone. . . . I'm my own worst critic. If I satisfy me,
> then everybody else is more than satisfied.

Because she was willing to put forth maximum effort, she expected faculty to do likewise. High expectations signified diligence and quality, both of which Mattie believed should constitute one's attitude toward work and learning. She expected that each part of an individual's work responsibilities would be carried out with care and accuracy, whether that meant filling out a report for the school or district office; completing the master schedule for a semester's classes; managing an athletic event with pride, respect, and dignity; or cleaning the cafeteria between lunch periods. She did not want to settle for less. She desired "the brightest, the most committed people who are positive, who have energy, who love people, who really want to do their jobs, [and] who are caring and nurturing."

Although Mattie perceived the striving for perfection as caring, not all the teachers did. They were accustomed to having their own way, choosing the manner in which they accomplished tasks, and not having to be overly concerned with anyone's perception of "quality." I did not ask whether they considered her standards as a step toward creating a caring climate, but I now wonder how many faculty members would have seen them as such.

Mattie did not want to settle for less where students were concerned, either. A hard-working faculty did not spend time solely preparing for classes and participating on school committees. High expectations for faculty must reflect high expectations for students. For Mattie, the latter included a belief in, and compassion for, students, as well as their actual academic achievement.

> I see caring for students in the sense that you have high expectations
> . . . believing that all students can and will learn. That you communi-
> cate with students . . . on a daily basis. . . . You're concerned if 50% of
> the students are not passing. And you don't immediately blame the stu-
> dent. . . . Showing that you care means that you're going to communi-
> cate with the parent, and the parent will become your ally, not your
> enemy. That you're going to join hands. You're going to ask, "What
> can I do?" You're going to show compassion. . . . You'll smile at the

student. . . . One can be strict . . . I believe in that, but one can set
those limits and one can do that in a very caring, compassionate way
and still get results. . . . [You] must truly feel that you can make a difference, and that you care about people, [that] you care about the students, really believe that they can learn, and want to make them learn.

With her commitment to care for students, Mattie asked teachers to stretch
more than many had in years. Did she really care about the teachers when she
asked them to think they could make a difference with students who rarely
came to school? Who lived lives that many of the teachers hurried to escape
when the final bell rang?

At the same time that she had high expectations of herself and others,
she was aware of her drive to be the best, a drive she saw as arising not only
from her innate personality, but because she was female. When I initially
questioned her about her position as the first *female* high school principal in
Newtown, she implied that as a women she was inclined to work harder and
longer in order to "prove" herself. She generalized that attitude to include
virtually all women in positions such as hers, and with ambitions to "climb
the executive ladder." Because she was aware of her tendency to push herself
to extremes, she had a personal goal of learning to delegate responsibility to
others. She hoped that would enable her to relinquish the need to be a
"superwoman," for, "women have to be very careful about being superpeople,
superwomen. We drive ourselves. I don't want to fall into that trap where I
feel that I must do it all."

Mattie seemed to understand that unless she cared for herself, she would
not be as capable of caring for staff, teachers, and students. Because she was
aware of the tendency to drive herself and, therefore, others, she had as a goal
for herself and her staff members to find and maintain a balance in life. To
her that meant having a life and an identity beyond DHS. Throughout the
year, she reiterated her struggle to find and maintain personal equilibrium.

She was frustrated with teachers who seemed to resist the notion of balance
in their lives, as she interpreted it. Her motives for desiring teachers to spend
less time involved in their jobs did not seem to arise solely out of care and
concern for them as persons, but out of concern, as principal, for their ability
to be the "brightest people" who had "energy to do their jobs."

If one has a family . . . [you need] time with your family. . . . When
people tell me they stay here . . . that does not guarantee quality. There
is only so much that human beings can do and you will wear yourself
out, become irritable, less productive. . . . I'm not impressed . . . when
people tell me that they're here until eight and nine o'clock. That

doesn't impress me because they can't last long. . . You want people with balance in their lives.

Mattie truly cared about the well-being of individual teachers. As a principal, however, she had to care for more than the individuals. She needed to nurture an entire school community. Therefore, by concerning herself with the need for teachers to have balance in their lives, she indicated an expediency necessary to care for the collective. There were too many substitute teachers in the building on a daily basis already; she wanted teachers to maintain emotional and physical health so they would contribute to the building, not deplete it of its resources. In that sense, she may not have been caring explicitly toward faculty, but about the school and all its constituents.

Accepting One's Humanity—Self and Others

Mattie appeared torn between wanting to be and do the best, and recognizing her own, as well as others', humanity, that is, the inevitability of being less than perfect. She said she was not a perfectionist, but she continually worked to accept that. As she talked about her humanity—the inescapable fact that she would make mistakes—she strived to acknowledge it in herself. Accepting less than perfection was not easy, especially as a woman making her way in the bureaucratic hierarchy.

> One of the things that I have learned to say is, "Yes, if you have any questions about whether or not a woman can be a high school principal, the answer is 'yes.'" I know that . . . I am not a superhuman being. I get tired, I hurt, my feelings can get [hurt], I make mistakes—all those things. . . . I want to be human. That human beings make mistakes because it is alright because all of us, if we live long enough, if we do anything, then we make a mistake.

Accepting one's humanity came with the expectation that if you made a mistake, you would acknowledge and learn from it. To Mattie, admitting your failure and taking responsibility for your actions, indicated your integrity and desire to improve. She included in "taking responsibility" the expectation that a person would find a way to correct her mistake, thus increasing her knowledge and competence. Mattie understood her responsibility as *allowing* people to make mistakes. She illustrated that at the beginning of the school year with reference to her deputy principal.

> My deputy just came to me and I had asked him to do something. I knew that he was new in that position. . . . He was supposed to have

gotten something in and didn't. Well, he is a human being. He said he had it and it got put in another stack, and that can happen. . . . But I want to use it now as a lesson for him. Now if that gets to be a pattern, then I have to speak to him about that. . . . [He needs to] find a way make his mistakes and learn from them.

Multiple and repeated errors, however, were not acceptable. As the year progressed, the deputy principal continued to have difficulty with several of his job responsibilities, chief of which was constructing the master schedule of classes for the second semester. I perceived the relationship between him and Mattie to lose all pretense of warmth and caring, and become one of forbearance and tolerance. Mattie's caring and concern focused on how the deputy's work affected those within Division High, and less on the feelings of the deputy per se.

Ministering to Faculty's and Students' Needs

Foundational to Mattie in the development of a school organization and climate that manifest caring was the necessity to minister to the needs of the people within. I specifically chose the word *minister*, because she described that aspect of her role as principal as "a calling." She did not choose it, but resigned herself to it, for the calling was "a gift that God has given me, that I should not shun, and that people see."

The "gift" to which she referred was her sensitivity toward the needs of others and her ability to listen to and counsel staff members. She viewed those as gifts because people sought her out for advice, comfort, and "just to talk." She put a high priority on making herself available to staff members experiencing personal difficulties—divorce, impending surgery, death in the family, or other family problems. Additionally, she interpreted her calling as being available to settle day-to-day disputes, frustrations, or misunderstandings among teachers. In her estimation, that calling required more of her time and energy than she had ever anticipated. At times she wrestled with what she expected of herself and what others expected of her as principal. Was she making the best choice when she opted to minister to staff in lieu of patrolling the halls or observing a classroom? She believed she was, for if "people are hurting and if I don't listen to them, then that is going to impact what happens to children in the classroom."

Right now we have about ten people who are going through some traumatic situations. . . . This is the part of the job that has been a real challenge. . . . A part of me want[s] to always be visible out there for students, but it can't always happen. [A] person called me and said, "I need to talk to *you*." I could pick up on the voice. So I had to switch gears. . . . Another individual asked me to give her time to explain something because what she wants is to have a conference with me and about five other staff members because something needs to be settled. Now that part is a biggy. . . . Most of what I do is listen. To listen takes time.

In every school, I'm sure there are teachers and students who must handle an array of personal problems. At Division High, however, many of the problems centered on violence, affecting teachers and students either directly or peripherally. Spousal abuse, drug-related incidents within families, and the murder and mugging of one teacher's relatives all occurred in barely half a school year. In addition, one teacher had open-heart surgery; another had cancer surgery and died unexpectedly of a heart attack; there were several natural deaths of parents and other relatives of staff members; and several spouses or close relatives of faculty had major surgery. Again, all this in less than a full school year. Add to this the traumatic events that occurred in the student body, and one began to wonder what "normal" was.

Besides listening, Mattie made programmatic changes to facilitate caring for those "who were hurting." Among her first acts as principal was to initiate grief counseling for students and for faculty. Within a month of school's starting, a student had been shot and killed. By January, three more students had died violently. Although the first incident put into practice what to her had been only vaguely thought-through ideas, she had known long before she was appointed chief administrator that grief counseling would be an integral part of "her" school.

Over the years, Mattie saw and experienced the trauma that students were expected to manage on their own. She also saw students hardening, that is, not allowing themselves to feel. That helped them cope with adversity, and, concomitantly, allowed them to lose hope for themselves and in their futures. The students accepted violence as an inevitable part of their lives and as something for which nothing could be done. Through grief counseling, Mattie opened up the possibility for students to question the violence and to allow themselves to recognize and perhaps feel their pain and anger. She wanted students to feel again. If they acknowledged their emotions, they could begin to think about a future for themselves. Ultimately, they might see that changing the life-style they thought was unchangeable was a possibility.

Mattie also understood that teachers needed help with their grief. Many of Division's faculty had taught there for 15 or more years. During that time, they witnessed and experienced the fury of desegregation: student riots, faculty battles, police brutality. From that time through the period of this study, each year teachers learned about a current or former student who was maimed or killed. One teacher noted that in 13 years, she had 12 students die violently. Like students, teachers tried to distance themselves from their grief by rationalizing the situations or by burying it within themselves because they had to teach their next class of 30-plus students.

At Mattie's former school, I observed a teacher who, at the beginning of class, was informed by a student that a male classmate had been shot the night before. The teacher, visibly shaken, tried to elicit more information about the shooting. The student flippantly replied that the young man had been dealing drugs and knew that would happen eventually. As the teacher continued trying to find out more details, the student seemed to have forgotten the incident and was more interested in who was doing what after school. The teacher, on the other hand, continued to ask questions, but eventually stopped as the students appeared disinterested in the incident and wanted to get on with the class. I talked with the teacher later in the day, and he told me that he had been teaching in the district for 25 years and no matter how many times he heard about a student's being hurt or killed, he was still shaken. But, he responded with resignation, what could one do about it except to go on and pretend it didn't happen?

Mattie's hope was that grief counseling would allow teachers to deal with their feelings so they did not have to pretend the incidents had not occurred. If teachers grieved, they might begin to feel with and for the students they taught, and students would begin to understand the grieving process. Paramount, however, was that through the grief process, teachers might begin to see students who were not simply troubled faces in their classes, but human beings with a future.

Mattie enthusiastically encouraged interested teachers to begin a program of crisis intervention with students. That program built on grief counseling. With the guidance of trained peers, students learned alternatives to fighting and violence to settle arguments and disagreements. Instead of physically fighting to resolve a verbal dispute, students were brought together in a room, mediated by peers, and instructed to talk out the disagreement until they came to consensus. If that did not occur within a session, another session was scheduled. According to Mattie, the teachers involved, and the student mediators, crisis intervention "worked" in virtually every case, preventing what otherwise would have resulted in beatings or worse.

Mattie spent time counseling students. She met with a senior and her grandparents to let them know the young lady was not excused from school that day. ("Girl, we got to get you graduated! . . . [Your grandparents] are working too hard. You need to graduate for them.") She performed crisis intervention with two boys who were on the verge of physical combat, but who left her office after shaking hands and apologizing to each other. She invited several students to a special luncheon to celebrate their academic achievement. She invited a young girl whose father had died to talk with her in her office. Those were but a few incidents that I observed. Students, as persons, were important to Mattie, and she tried to make time to listen to them.

Ministering to faculty's and students' needs was critical to Mattie's understanding of her role as a caring principal. As she said, "Most people really want to be validated as worthwhile human beings. To care about them. It does not take much. You can't be superficial about it, but you just genuinely care."

Building Community

Mattie's "ministering" now became her "ministry." Her most important goal in the community was to visit the neighborhood churches that served Division's students. She met with the local Concerned Pastors' Council[6] to arrange to visit their congregations during designated Sunday services. During those times, she discussed the need for support from the church as a body, and the parishioners as individual parents and community members, to help improve Division High for students. Her pleas to the congregations ranged from financial aid and the need for volunteer help at the school, to the need for parents and community members to convince students of the importance of education and to encourage them to stay in school.

Mattie worked to bolster sagging participation and attendance of the parent advisory council. She encouraged the liaison between the school and community to sponsor events that would bring parents to the school. One such event was a breakfast in May for students entering ninth grade in the fall and their parents. The purpose was to meet teachers, counselors, and selected students. Mattie advertised—through the media, through the churches, through letters to parents, and through word of mouth—the open house for parents and students in the fall; it had the largest turnout in years. Teachers, used to spending 4 hours at an open house to see five to ten parents wander through, witnessed more than 100 the first semester Mattie was at DHS. Mattie asked the journalism teacher to start a newsletter for parents. It contained information about happenings in the school generally, notices from specific teachers, and details concerning major events or requirements that affected students. Parents received such a letter several times throughout the year. Finally, Mattie always seemed to be available to parents—sometimes to teachers' annoyance.

Of the five goals that Mattie had at the beginning of the year, improving school–community relations was the one that she declared she had achieved, and to a much higher degree than she had anticipated. During my final interview with her, she commented:

> I expected cooperation, but I did not expect it to the degree that I received it. Just outstanding to the degree that [parents] would call and ask, "Now what can we do to help? What can we do?" They have been supportive all along by their presence and by their money. . . . It's just a comforting feeling to know that you have the community backing you. You see you're not in it alone.

Unlike her assessment of having to struggle for teachers' help, Mattie felt that the parents and community cooperated and collaborated with her. She seemed to feel the reciprocity of caring in her relationship with the community.

REFLECTIONS ON MATTIE'S UNDERSTANDINGS OF CARING

Mattie's caring was intense and personal. It was much like Noddings suggests. Mattie attempted to understand, to get into the skin of, others in order to understand how to care for them. Mattie saw herself as care-giver to staff and students. She felt their need for caring and was determined to do all that she could to be nurturing and sensitive. She took her call to minister seriously.

Mattie, however, had difficulty receiving care from others within the school. At times she reflected Noddings's perception of the one caring who may, at the same time, be the one receiving care. That is, there were times that Mattie's attempts to care for someone were really cries to be cared-for. In a new position in which she was uncomfortable dealing with ambiguity and often feeling she had only limited control, her acts of caring, at times, resulted in others allowing her to care for them. She, then, felt cared-for, that is, she felt competent and, in a sense, in control.

Mattie as care-receiver was a difficult, if not an impossible, role for her to choose to play. She indicated that she often felt alone and isolated, that she had one very good friend with whom she could really talk, and that she felt the need to build a network among the female secondary school principals at the regional conference. Never, though, did she indicate that she believed there was a possibility of receiving care from staff members. She had genuine concern that she did not have as much control of her situation as a new principal as much as she thought she should have. That disturbed her and seemed to make her feel not only uncomfortable, but less than competent. *She* was there to lead and to minister, not to be ministered to.

Caring, for Mattie, also seemed to mean attention to the maintenance of bureaucracy. She ultimately was the leader and therefore was responsible for the success or failure of the school. Building trust, pride, and community not only were caring toward individuals, but were potentially the means by which DHS could regain respect within the district hierarchy and educational community. Although she talked of working together with the faculty—of collaborating—she made the decisions regarding who would collaborate and when.

Caring seemed to involve her vision and how it could be accomplished within the bureaucracy that she seemed to understand and respect. While I continued to see caring and power as binary opposites, she seemed comfortable using both together.

CHAPTER 5

The Principal: Caring Power?

[In a letter to a student and friend] Wittgenstein insisted that, as difficult as it was to "think well about 'certainty,' 'probability,' 'perception,'" it was "still more difficult to think or try to think, really honestly about your life and other people's lives. And the trouble is that thinking about these things is not thrilling, and often downright nasty. And when it's nasty then it's most important."
—Jean B. Elshtain, *Power Trips and Other Journeys*, 1990

Mattie wanted to be known as nurturing, caring, and understanding, a "people person." There was another very important part of her, however. Faculty and staff liked her, as some of them said, because she was a "take-charge," "no-nonsense" person, and because she was firm in her beliefs and did not fear taking strong positions on issues. Mattie appreciated her own preparedness, organization, and ability to set goals and develop plans to achieve them. She valued herself as others saw her—in control.

Through the years she perceived herself very much a leader—one who had vision, knew how to pursue it, and nurtured and encouraged staff to attain it. As a principal with the mission to create a school *community*, she struggled with the meaning of leadership aimed to be community-oriented and committed to shared decision-making, collaboration, and interdependence of staff and administration. At times, she seemed to wrestle with her beliefs in control and authority, ingrained through years of training and currently imposed on her by others (superintendent, board of education, university, business community, and faculty), and with her desire and commitment to caring. Those struggles, however, did not prevent her from using the power of her position to make unilateral decisions, to limit or initiate projects, and to set a course for the school while the faculty labored to cooperate in order to develop their vision. Her taking charge often caused teachers and staff to question her use of power over them. Yet, she seemed to believe that using power was necessary to establish an atmosphere in which caring flourished.

I began to question the polarization of caring and power. Are caring and power mutually exclusive, that is, is it possible to "be in control" and to care simultaneously? Is it necessary to have *power over* in order to achieve a cultural

64

climate and organizational structure that support caring, or is that notion an oxymoron?

Thinking about Mattie in relation to power that connoted authority or control, was not as easy for me as seeing her in relation to caring. The power relationship did not seem as clean or as unambiguous for me. As I contemplated that thought, I realized that a key component in my assessment of her caring was her awareness of *wanting* to be caring, of her *talking* about herself as caring, of her *recognizing* the importance caring had in her conception of herself as a leader, and of her *believing* that caring among staff and students was critical for good teaching and learning to occur. Power, on the other hand, was not mentioned; neither was authority or control. Power, implying authority or control, was only indirectly addressed as accountability or responsibility in conjunction with her role as building administrator. However, she did assume power through her position.

I began to see Mattie as conflicted by having to "give up" power because of the quest to develop shared decision-making and management with others. I assumed she believed that relinquishing control was necessary to establish caring and willingly struggled to "let go."

Unlike her straightforward, confident talk about, and acts of, caring, her use of 'power over' manifested itself in seemingly uneven and, sometimes, unexpected ways. At times she seemed to stand straight and tall, wielding power like a magnificent protectress of The Good; at other times, she seemed to be buffeted by the power of others, never fully losing control but fighting to maintain her balance. Perhaps she did not see power in caring as an issue; one could care and be powerful simultaneously, for one used power not for one's own aggrandizement, but to uplift those who had less, or no, power.

Despite the unevenness, she tended to frame her use and pursuit of power in an ethic of caring. Mattie saw control and authority not as ends in themselves, but as ways to gain ground in her efforts to build communication and trust; to achieve high expectations, integrity, and community; and to minister to individuals—to realize her desire for a school and district where people were committed to caring for each other. As she strove to create an ethic of caring in the school community, she simultaneously prepared her way to "move up" within the traditional hierarchy.

TAKING POWER—WORKING WITH EXTERNAL FORCES

To most people, Mattie's appointment as principal could not have been more welcome. It seemed as though everyone, the staff and neighborhood community, as well as outside groups, believed in and supported her. She inherited two newly formed partnerships dedicated to transforming DHS into a model school. A local business group volunteered to work with students and teachers, financing innovative educational projects and mentoring students in business classes. Additionally, a major university sought to collaborate via the Professional Development School model to improve teaching and learning. With support from within the school community and from without, how could she fail?

If Mattie were a poker player, she might have said that her year began with a full house. But, instead, the house was built *of* cards, standing on a weak foundation and precariously balanced. The outsiders saw—or chose to see—only the facade, targeting their efforts at strengthening portions that appeared weak and would exhibit visible improvement. Mattie, however, was concerned about the foundation and about the development and quality of the whole design. Thus begins the story of my struggle to understand Mattie's use of power as a caring leader.

Because she inherited the partnerships with the university and business groups, she also inherited their expectations. Their aspirations emanated primarily from three sources: their initial contacts with the previous principal, their own assessments and assumptions about Division, and their own needs.

Mattie appeared to put as much effort into keeping the university and business groups, the outsiders, at arm's length as she did into building relationships with the community and staff. She seemed to fear a "take-over" by them. Although she thought their intentions were sincere, she also believed that there was a reality of which they and her staff were either unaware or did not want to face. Persons from the university and from the business community were outsiders who had limited understanding of the school and of the impact that its history had on the present. Their offers of money and help to teachers beleaguered by a lack of resources and burdened by the citizenry's negative perception of DHS, their expectations of immediate and dramatic change, and their assumptions that the DHS staff would want and need the same changes they thought necessary, caused her to fear another round of school reform that would do nothing more than increase the patchwork that already existed. Because many faculty members desperately wanted to make positive changes for students, they viewed those offers of help uncritically. Mattie, therefore, used her authority as principal to control the changes within the school, and the rate at which they occurred, in order to give staff the time to identify their own and the school's needs. The university and the business groups both indicated they wanted to work *with* Division High, and Mattie wanted to be sure that happened.

> We are going to have to work out some things with [the university] . . . so that we are upfront with each other and we can work together. Things are going to evolve and with everything it takes time. . . . Staff

members will determine how much and how soon. [It's] a very good program, good things started, but you can't push; it does take time.

Throughout the year, Mattie emphasized that as much as the outside groups wanted to help, there were pressing issues within the school that needed the staff's and her attention. Unless those groups could understand that, their "help" would be nothing more than a hindrance. Consequently, Mattie continued, as many faculty interpreted it, to drag her feet—or even dig her heels in, according to some—to prevent major changes from occurring too rapidly and without proper forethought and planning. She wanted to stop the *idea* of change from luring staff—and, ultimately, students—into a rocketing roller coaster ride of superficial programs that quickly rose and just as quickly plunged into oblivion.

The longer you are here, you will understand some of the in-house things that we are going to have to work out. We cannot deal with the pressures from without until we are ready. There are staff members that are ready. They want to use the resources. . . . [But] you can't push. One of the things that you and I both know [is] that there have been many good programs that are in what I call the education graveyard because we didn't prepare the market for them, we did not assess. It does take time.

Since I was involved with the university–school partnership, Mattie visited with me, formally and informally, regarding the university's role at DHS. She recognized that Division needed assistance in order to make the magnitude of changes she envisioned, and that the partnership with the university had the potential to contribute to an improved school organization and curriculum.

The idea of a collaborative effort was appealing to her. However, she also believed that no individual, or organization, was truly altruistic: If something was given, something was sought in return. She sensed that the university team came with an agenda of its own. That in itself was not offensive. The problem was that it was unspoken. There was a contradiction in terms. The university entered Division with the intent of *collaboratively* working to improve the school. Implied was that teachers and members of the university team would share information and work together, shoulder to shoulder, to discover what Division had and needed. Instead, the university folks *told* her and the staff about Division's needs.

Collaboration, she concluded, was not occurring. Rather, she observed the distrust that some teachers had for the university–school partnership concept, and that nothing was being done by the university to allay that distrust. She perceived disorganization when university team members were unable to supply her with what seemed like obvious information—what was happening with the projects involving DHS teachers and the team, or who was going to be in the building at particular times. She observed unclear goals for the university–school effort when she received contradictory statements from various team members.

For 5 months after her appointment as principal, the university faculty treated Mattie as the invisible black woman. No one from the university contacted her to discuss strategies for working together. No one from the university informed her of the work with faculty that had been done to date. No university faculty members even paid her the courtesy of introducing themselves until mid-October, 6 weeks after school began and 5-1/2 months after they had begun working with DHS teachers. Although Mattie made no mention of that, a close colleague inferred that Mattie felt she had been ignored primarily because she was black. According to her friend, Mattie believed the university staff expected her to be thrilled with their attentions and help. The friend's perception was that Mattie was a pawn to reflect kudos on them for helping a black female principal put this poor, urban school "on track."

Whether or not the colleague's interpretation was accurate, the university's treatment of Mattie was an affront to her personally and professionally. It was obvious to me that Mattie struggled to remain dignified and professional as she entered into an inherited school–university partnership with partners whose behavior was arrogant and unprofessional.

Throughout the year, Mattie continued to feel a lack of professional respect and collegiality as university team members came in with their pre-planned agenda. Despite the collaboration rhetoric, they, like myriad school reformers of the past, would use the school to accomplish tasks important to their goals. She did not perceive attempts to understand her role as principal, nor did she experience their appreciation for her position as a *new* principal. (Although Mattie would not expect this, I would add that there was no appreciation of her ground-breaking role in Newtown as the first *female* high school principal.)

> I think that we ought to be excited about . . . the theme [that] people are now willing to come and join hands and work together, but you can't have a driving force. People will push back. You cannot have that plan already mapped out and say, "Now here it is. You fit around it." It just won't work. As a new principal, there is just so much I have to learn. So much I have to get under my belt and [I] just don't need any bickering, any pulling, or pushing or prodding. That is not what I had in mind when we looked at any group coming in. You want to help. What I said to staff is, on the other hand, "Now keep in mind when people spend their time and money, they must have a say in

what is to take place. That is the other side of it." All of it takes time.
. . . We have to communicate and keep our eyes open and be very sensitive to a whole history for this particular school.

Mattie also had concerns about the school's partnership with the local business group. The representative committee came with good intentions, but with limited knowledge regarding the functioning of schools generally and Division High specifically. Prior to Mattie's becoming principal, the committee proposed to fund DHS teachers for innovative projects and/or to assist in projects just underway. Participants were to outline their projects/activities, giving the purpose, student outcomes, and a detailed account of the needed resources, including funding. Several teachers saw the offer as a way to involve students in activities that would strengthen their understandings of a particular subject area and that were previously unavailable due to lack of funds. Some teachers envisioned larger organizational changes—schools within a school—to better serve students. Others imagined ways to restructure classes to better meet their own needs, and to purchase desired equipment. How the individual proposals would support the overall mission of the school, or fit into the overall curriculum, received little, if any, faculty consideration. In some cases, the proposals were quite self-serving, having no sound academic basis for students and no clear student outcomes. The committee, however, approved all proposals if they met financial limits and reasonable time lines and outcomes according to business standards.

Mattie noted that several of the proposed changes had merit for the long term. However, proposals requiring major changes appeared so quickly that not enough time and thought were given to how they *all* fit into the total picture of Division High. Because of the business group's offers of funding, the pace set for change exceeded Mattie's comfort level. She wanted the staff to consider their goals for the school as a whole; that is, Mattie saw a need for individual teachers to think beyond their own wants and desires to the articulation of each project into the existing programs and projected goals for student learning. She did not see that happening.

The principal perceived the business group's offer of money as a signal for the faculty, who were conditioned to function with minimal resources, to swiftly generate proposals, regardless of their pedagogical and academic soundness and regardless of how the projects or activities articulated with other classes, courses, or undertakings. She sensed a feeling of urgency among the staff, as though the funding they would receive depended on the alacrity—not quality—with which they submitted their proposals. Mattie feared that some faculty members viewed money as the primary factor involved in making changes and failed to acknowledge the time, effort, and commitment to overall transformation that were needed.

People see money as a way of doing all of these things, not recognizing that it takes time and it takes hard work, and . . . you build a foundation and move from there. And that has not happened. . . . So, therefore, there were those who wanted to take advantage of the fact that we'll take your money, but we won't be accountable for anything. And that concerned me.

Mattie focused on systematic and systemic change, keeping in mind the "big picture," the ways in which each new idea would affect the total school. Representatives of the business community infringed on that process. In fact, Mattie viewed the university and business groups as further fragmenting the staff and programs, rather than fostering collaboration. Their offers of funding and other material and human resources, although not undesirable, were another hurdle put in her way of working with faculty.

She sensed the outside groups, although perhaps well-intentioned, were not, as she liked to say, "singing from the same hymn book" as she was. That is, they were operating at their own cadence and in tune to their own needs. The staff divided even more, and tension between Mattie and the staff increased, as the outside groups overlapped in their work with faculty yet functioned independently of each other and, in essence, of DHS.

Limited communication, at best, took place between the groups. The communication that did exist occurred between the management levels of the groups. Within the university team, the people who actually worked with the teachers rarely were privy to the information exchanged at the higher levels of the bureaucracy. Lack of communication caused misunderstandings between school staff and representatives of each of the outside sources, as faculty often heard one thing from one group and another from the other. Like deprived children, some teachers tried to play one group against the other to garner the most resources and/or support, or to exert pressure on the other group—or Mattie—for their particular project. Mattie felt squeezed in the middle of two feuding "helpers."

But I also had [the university] and, at the same time, the [local business group] . . . each not quite sure about each other and not quite sure about their agendas. That was overwhelming [to me] at first. It was a surprise, the . . . disagreement over turf. . . . I saw that [the university] and the [local business group] were pulling at each other and not clear, not comfortable with each other. . . . I believe that I was going to have to say some things very clearly to both. That you have to get your acts together because we're [Division High] getting caught in the middle, and staff can see that.

Given the above situations with the university and business partnerships, I determined that Mattie had two choices: either conform to their wishes and take what they offered—Division High did need the resources, and the teachers were eager to cooperate—or resist and, perhaps, risk losing the resources and possibly her support from some faculty members. The latter action would effectively acknowledge a struggle between Mattie and the outside groups for control over—for power over—the changes made at DHS. That, in effect, would determine the future direction of the school and its leadership. The latter action also had the potential to set up a power struggle between Mattie and the faculty. Mattie chose to resist while simultaneously seeking to establish common ground whereby the university, business groups, and school would benefit. Mattie attempted to use her power to slow the pace of change to bring about outcomes satisfactory to the outside groups and, more important for her, to give her and the DHS staff time to determine what *they* really needed.

Mattie resisted not by overtly opposing the outsiders' ideas for change, but by resisting their impositions and implicit demands. She attended meetings called by the groups, particularly by the university, only at her convenience and then rarely, if ever, staying for the entire time. She stipulated rules determining her participation in the partnerships, particularly the university, and ignored situations or "obligations" that did not meet those rules. She allowed people, including her own teachers, to "spin their wheels" on projects she did not want begun at that time by encouraging them to work on their ideas and to get faculty support for them, while she stood passively by. The effect, despite support from external groups, was either to dramatically limit the speed at which changes occurred, or to sound the death-knell for projects she seemingly chose not to support.

I saw Mattie's resistance as a declaration of power—of her power to determine what, if any, influence the university and business groups would have at DHS. I perceived her silently announcing, so all could hear, that the right to change Division High School would remain with those who were a part of it—teachers, students, administrators, and parents. It appeared that she saw the need to exert power—authority and control—in order to someday effect caring.

The themes of hidden agendas and of expecting too much too soon permeated Mattie's conversation from October through June. Having to deal with two external groups added to the strain of learning her role and of striving to bring the staff together to determine the goals for Division High. The university and local business groups demanded—not asked for—her time, her assistance, her cooperation—and her appreciation. There was an implicit assumption within each of the groups that they would determine what was best for DHS and they therefore would orchestrate the needed changes. Mattie, however, believed otherwise: She and the staff knew DHS and therefore *they* would establish and pursue their own goals at their own speed. If the external groups truly wanted to assist, they had to learn to collaborate with her and the staff; they needed to make the effort to get to know the community of Division High School.

> We're going to do this [participate in changes with help from the university and the business community] slowly. [When] we're talking about a real change . . . it's going to take time. . . . If [the university people] are going to be here, if they're truly committed to [helping DHS], and if they're talking about change, it's not going to be done [immediately]. . . . We will start to see some real things by the time I leave here. . . . I've said the same thing to the [business community committee]. You see, what has really hurt is that some people had some agendas before they came here, and that's not going to work. . . . So we will determine what it is that we want— people, resources—to do. . . . What does the school need? . . . If you come already with a set of [changes] it will not work. *It will not work* [emphasis hers]. . . . We have to assess what it is that we're doing now. [And] teachers, those who work in those classrooms, will determine [that]. . . . The portion that bothers me is there's not enough time. That's a serious mistake for [the university] to come in and think it's going to happen overnight. That was a real concern when I came in, as I've said before, that someone was expecting miracles. . . . So, having the goals of learning about the community—the community meaning the students, the staff—talking to everyone one on one, and getting a sense of purpose and mission, should also be the goal [of the university].

Mattie used her authority to "protect" DHS from the power of those external to the school system and community. There was no question in her mind that she was responsible for the future of that building and would do all in her power to maintain control over the school. If Mattie perceived the collaboration as mainly rhetoric, perhaps she saw no other recourse than to use "power over" until the others could hear her well enough to talk *with* her and not *at* her. She did not seem to be compromised by her use of control and authority, viewing them as the means by which she could fend off forces that had the potential to undermine her goal of establishing Division High as a school that was fundamentally a place where its people were cared for.

MAINTAINING POWER—BALANCING SCHOOL AND DISTRICT BUREAUCRATIC EXPECTATIONS

Working within the building's and school district's bureaucratic systems presented a different set of concerns for Mattie regarding power. Unlike her confident use of "power over" with groups external to the school system, she appeared to be uncertain about her use of "power over" with those within the system. Her uncertainty arose, perhaps, from the effects of her past on the present. Throughout her career as an educator, Mattie prepared herself to be a high school principal by observing traditional administrators whom she admired and by accepting mentorship as it was offered. Qualities she took pride in included being highly organized, being well prepared, leaving nothing to chance, accepting responsibility and accountability for what happened within the school, and having respect for the authority that came with position in the hierarchy. Those characteristics, she believed, would enable her to be an effective leader, one who confidently made decisions unilaterally or who orchestrated the conditions by which she and others made them.

When she became principal, the role as she always had envisioned it no longer existed, but neither was there a new model for her to follow. Division High had become a site-based managed school with shared decision-making. Although the meaning and implementation of those concepts were not clearly defined, the general understanding among staff was that school management and policy making would be shared among many, with the principal as only one among the many. Mattie's job, therefore, was to make the transition between "the leader" and "leadership by many," personally as well as professionally. Making the transition required her to share leadership, yet to be accountable to the district for the happenings and decisions made within the school. She encountered several dilemmas: How much authority and control did she exert in order to find how much she needed to give up? How much decision-making, and with whom, was she willing to share when she alone was held responsible to the district hierarchy? How did site-based management and shared decision-making in one school work in a system that operated hierarchically? For Mattie, there was "nothing more difficult to take in hand, more perilous of conduct, or more uncertain in its success" than facing a new principalship at a school shifting to site-based management and shared decision-making.

From the beginning, site-based management had not been enthusiastically supported by the majority of DHS's administrators and staff. Immediately prior to Mattie's appointment as principal, the superintendent proposed that the school consider reorganizing to become site-based. Much discussion ensued for no one really understood what SBM would look like. The understandings ranged from some teachers' view that teachers would have total control of the building, to others' view that teachers would make the decisions and administrators would carry them out. Still others saw SBM as something in between—teachers, support staff, parents, and students working together to make and implement decisions.

After two votes of the entire staff, SBM was approved as the organizational structure of choice. The first vote showed that administrators, as well as many staff members, were not in favor of that change in organization; the second vote, according to some teachers, did not really change matters, except there was pressure from "downtown" for DHS to become a site-based managed school. Therefore, administrators felt they had little choice but to vote in favor of adopting SBM, for becoming site-based managed was conditional on administrative support.

Although several teachers speculated that Mattie did not favor SBM, she stated otherwise. She did not, however, embrace it without reservations and frustration. Administrators from the district office informed her that there were guidelines for the district's goals and expectations for SBM in individual buildings—although each school with SBM was to be unique and to develop SBM to suit its own purposes. She did not know who developed the guidelines or how, and she had not seen them as of the end of the school year. She vacillated between her loyalty to the hierarchy and her frustration with the spoken and implied expectations.

> We're not there yet [concerning SBM]. I think the district probably has not helped, [but] I'm not being critical of it. . . . [SBM's] so new and . . . the district has said, "Well, now, you go and you decide how you're going to operate. You don't have to be the same as [X] High School. Or you don't have to have the same as [Y]." And that's good, and yet it can cause some confusion. So, right now, I'm not comfortable with how we operate. . . . No one has given me those guidelines.

Confusion also resulted from the lack of common understanding about SBM among teachers and administrators throughout the district, and what could be expected through such school reorganization. Mattie, midway through the year, reflected that after a year and a half of working with the concept of SBM, the school was still not site-based. There were expectations from the district administration of which faculty either were not aware or had lost sight; the roles of the steering committee members, including administrators, were unclear; and the specific course of action for the school had not been determined.

> What we have going on now is not truly site-based. As the district defines it, it has to be focused on student achievement. You have some misunderstanding in terms of what [SBM is]. . . . I mean that's to be expected. But we have to first define what it is. The other thing we have to do is determine what the role of the steering committee, our governance board, will be. . . . I see confusion. I see people really not having a full understanding.

Although there were no guidelines from the district for making the transition to SBM, Mattie believed her "bosses" had some ideas regarding the process—they may not have been able to explain it, but they would know it when they saw it happening. The expectations were murky. Rather than being continually prepared and organized, and knowing the direction she wanted to take for DHS, Mattie found herself having to come to grips with ambiguity in her new role.

> If I have to say that I have a skill, a talent, [it] is that I'm not a last minute person. I do try to stay ahead. But all of us come short, and I'm uncomfortable right now because normally I'm more on top of things and I know why I'm not because this is all new. . . . I finally, as principal, had to settle and resign myself to know that, when you come in [new], and when . . . change is going to occur, things are so unsettled at first.

There was ambiguity resulting from the lack of clarity in her role during and after the transition to SBM. As the building principal, she continued to see herself as the final authority, the one who was responsible for all that occurred within the school; she referred to Division as "her" building. What happened at Division was a direct reflection on her as a professional and as a person. In addition, her personal feelings of responsibility were supported by the district administrators' very real expectations of *her* accountability to them for the management of Division. The result was a division within herself. "Being in charge" was contradictory to the "shared" leadership espoused by SBM and the concept of shared decision-making. "Being in charge" connoted "power over," that is, control and authority. "Shared" leadership connoted "empowerment" or "caring." Mattie felt caught in the middle between traditional beliefs and understandings of leadership, and an emerging, yet murky, vision of shared leadership; between the past and the future.

> You put a person in charge [with SBM] and yet, that's somewhat contradictory of the whole notion of site-based management. But, I do know I have a sense of being [held] responsible, and how I know that is I get the telephone calls. . . . And when something has not been turned in, site-based or not, . . . I get the call. And, so . . . I know that some things have not changed. I get the feeling that the principal is held accountable.

Mattie continually checked with her "boss" to make sure she was on track with SBM and that the district administration expected no more than DHS accomplished. Although frustrated because of the contradictory position created by the district administration, she was supportive and loyal to her "bosses." She looked to her immediate supervisor, the Director of Secondary Education, for guidance and backing, and repaid him with respect and loyalty. She did not question his authority and accepted having to "pay my dues" as a newcomer in her position, in order to earn the respect and authority from those above her.

Conversely, SBM caused conflict between Mattie and some teachers, especially those who were strong unionists. Recall the history of anti-administration sentiment escalated by strong union influence. Active union members dominated the steering committee, the governance body of SBM, from its inception at the school. Mattie—and many teachers—felt the teachers' union pushed for SBM as a way to take over the schools. However, few unionist steering committee members viewed SBM as a way to gain control of the school, nor did most want to.[7] The attitude of the few who may have felt that way, however, prompted Mattie to act in ways leaving no doubt about who was in authority and backing the district's right to mandate Division's compliance—SBM or not—with policy.

Mattie became impatient with teachers' notions and talk about site-based management and shared decision-making as solely a mechanism through which they might gain more, or most, control of the school. Despite the district's ambiguous *process* of SBM, she did believe in the district's reasoning behind it: to improve student achievement.

> The whole notion of site-based is focused on student achievement. Now what it is not, is . . . not managing the building. . . . All of our endeavors with regard to site-based and shared decision-making has to be focused on this, on student achievement, what it is that we want to do to make learning . . . better for students in the classroom. . . . We have to have a common vision, which we don't.

Mattie, on the other hand, seemed to treat the steering committee of SBM cavalierly, attending meetings at her convenience and with little communication to members regarding when and why she would not be in attendance. Only the chair knew whether or when she would be present. Although another administrator represented her in her absence, the teachers felt that was insufficient, for the representative had virtually no authority to speak for her. The primary purpose of SBM—improving student learning—consequently was derailed by topics that focused on the process of SBM and by the need for decisions to settle teacher–administrator disputes over building control. Mattie's response to teacher disgruntlement was that she could not be at all meetings and therefore delegated others to attend in her absence; she fulfilled her obligation. When she chose to attend a district athletic meeting over a steering committee meeting, however, hostility escalated among those very people with whom she said she wanted to build trust.

As much as Mattie maintained a "power over" position in relation to SBM, she struggled to understand how to share power through the development of her role and the teachers' roles in the transition to SBM. She cited as progress the proposal that developed the mechanism by which faculty could initiate changes through SBM. She recognized the lack of role definition within SBM, and that, specifically, her role on the steering committee was nebulous. The latter was a problem. While staff members looked to her for direction, thus preserving her authority, she simultaneously garnered hostility for not allowing teachers to make decisions independent of her.

Several teachers considered teacher control of the budget, sans staff salaries, as an integral part of SBM. On numerous occasions, including the steering committee retreat,[8] teachers requested that Mattie share the budget with them. Mattie consistently said she did not have that information or did not have an adequate understanding of the budget process to share it with the committee. As the year progressed, teachers continued to ask about the budget, but narrowed their requests until they asked only about the money taken in from the pop machines. Mattie promised she would provide that information to the steering committee. At the end of the school year, the committee did not have it.

Budget information was a touchy subject for Mattie, one that was intricately connected to her integrity, her relationship to the district office, and her knowledge of past history at Division High. A past principal had been accused of embezzling funds from several sources within the school. Although the incident was covered up, the principal was removed from his position at DHS and transferred to another position where he could be monitored more easily. Veteran teachers recall the incident quite vividly.

Mattie never mentioned the incident to me, nor, to my knowledge, did she discuss it with members of the steering committee. She quite emphatically linked her integrity to her accountability, however, especially as it related to budgetary matters and the steering committee. Also, she emphatically refused to communicate to the steering committee or any group of teachers the budget information they requested. There was no doubt in anyone's mind, especially Mattie's, that teachers would not have control of the budget unless she was so instructed by her superiors.

> The one thing that I cannot give up at this moment . . . is this business
> of financial matters. That will kill credibility, that will kill us. Well,
> that will kill me. . . . Integrity is important to me. It's so very impor-
> tant and I just know when you start to deal with money matters, that
> if it's not handled correctly—and that's a big one—a lot of things are

going on in a school in a lot of ways and right now, I cannot turn that [budget] over to a committee of people yet. . . . There has to be an accounting . . . making sure that every penny goes where it's supposed to go when it's supposed to go. . . . And I'm more conscious of that, I guess, because of how I feel about integrity. And money can tear up a church; it can tear up a family. . . . Although our mission is to deal with students and what happens with students, and that's where I truly feel that I want to impact. . . . *But, money matters!* [emphasis hers]

In reality, site-based management and shared decision-making were imposed on DHS and therefore on Mattie. With the exception of building community through her church contacts and with parents, her other goals were overshadowed by the time and effort she spent on SBM. Although Mattie believed in collaboration and shared decision-making, I question whether she would have chosen SBM as the method by which to implement them.

[My] actually learning [about] and pushing site-based, shared decision-making . . . demand a lot more time than I had expected. . . . It's a lot of work. And if anyone thinks that it [site-based management, shared decision-making] isn't more work, then you're barking up the wrong tree. . . . Site-based, shared decision-making, I believe in it. I believe that it can work and it's my personal philosophy, but it does take a lot of time. . . . One surprise that I had, I had to back off because of the amount of time that it was taking.

Within the district bureaucracy, Mattie's commitment to the establishment of a caring community often became subsumed in the maintenance of the power of her position. She had to handle the expectations, stated and implied by district administrators, for her to develop site-based management in DHS. She struggled to retain a vision of herself as a competent administrator, while acknowledging she was in the midst of changes testing her abilities to deal with instability, ambiguity, and continual challenges to her authority. Lastly, she realized she must attend to her understanding that, as a woman, she felt the tendency to drive herself to prove herself worthy of being the first female high school principal in Newtown. All of those situations tested—and compromised—her power to build a caring community for Division High.

PURSUING POWER—CLIMBING THE HIERARCHICAL LADDER

At the same time Mattie pursued a course leading to the creation of an ethic of caring within Division High, she also was cognizant of her own power to earn the respect of her peers. The latter, she hoped, would broaden her scope of authority and allow her to advance in the hierarchy of the school district. People have a tendency to view the establishment of one's own power as simply self-serving and at the expense of others. Conversely, the establishment of an ethic of caring implies that one acts out of altruism and that "power over" is virtually absent. Mattie's case was not nearly so clear-cut. As she strove to build relationships and to nurture faculty and students, she also strove to further herself.

Mattie's goal was to become a high school principal. She worked her way into that position, moving up the career ladder one step at a time. Arriving at her goal, however, did not mean that she was content to simply *be* principal. Although she did not evidence any ambition to become a district administrator, many of the faculty speculated that her position at DHS was a stepping stone in that direction. Whether or not that was the case, Mattie knew she needed to build her power base as a principal in the district and in the region—she wanted to be an influence among her peers.

As she reflected on her first regional secondary school principals' meeting, she commented that because there were so few females in the organization, she had to be aware of networking with the males. Her inclination was to arrive at the meetings in time only to comfortably get settled before the business actually began. She learned, however, that if she wanted to have an impact on that group, she would have to leave her work at DHS, arriving at the site early in order to "visit" with others prior to the meeting. Choosing to build her political network took her away from the building, which had the consequence of decreasing the amount of time she spent with faculty and staff building the one-on-one relationships she believed were so important.

There were two driving forces behind Mattie's decision to network. The first was to gain support on a wider basis for the need to build trust, not only in her school, but among schools. Trust was important to teachers' and administrators' ability to collaborate and share ideas and thoughts about ways to better educate students. The second was that she could better "climb the executive ladder."

Mattie worked hard to build her power base within the district by working closely with her "bosses" and with the community. By doing that, she garnered support from them for grief counseling for students and teachers, for the student crisis intervention program, and for academic honors convocations for students. There was also speculation that her growing reputation in the district and community led to significant input into the selection of principals to fill the vacancies occurring in the district because of the early retirement buy-out. At least seven of the people who applied for the vacancies were from either DHS or her former school, and of those seven, four were female. They were people that Mattie mentored or who were closely allied to her through their similar values and beliefs concerning education.

For Mattie, power and caring mingled, integrated, and became inextricably entwined. She was a powerful care-giver.

MATTIE JOHNSON—POWERFUL CARE-GIVER

As I listened to the tape of the December interview with Mattie, the strain in her voice was evident. My field notes indicated that in answering my question concerning her perceptions about the changes faculty wanted at DHS and whether or not they saw any, Mattie became very serious and all business. She appeared uncomfortable—perhaps even fighting defensiveness—having to admit that everything was not running smoothly and that, although she did not like it, she had to learn to function in a position and a situation that were not clearly defined. When she told me early in September that "once I get through this year, then I can know more of what to expect," her smile and ebullient laugh implied that she could not believe that she would not always have a clear direction in sight.

The pressure she felt manifested itself visibly in her look, her stance, and her voice. This once ebullient woman, with a laugh that resounded throughout the building, became more tense and controlled as the months progressed. When I listened to the tape again, I felt myself tighten and become almost frightened in response to the intensity of her voice. I could recall sitting in her office. Although her posture was normally dignified, she now appeared to me to be stiff, rigid, steely-willed, and immovable. Anger—perhaps frustration—seemed to boil within her, but, because of her enormous self-control, it was translated into carefully monitored statements and responses. She exhibited power—to fight for an ethic of caring? The spontaneous, genuine smiles became "proper" smiles, and her eyes were hard and set.

Reflections on Mattie's Understandings of Power

Mattie's education in leadership principles and behaviors occurred in the bureaucratic setting of school. She rose through the hierarchy—teacher, department chairperson, assistant principal, deputy principal, and finally principal. Her former principal mentored her. She learned to lead, to take charge, to make decisions, and to take responsibility for her decisions. She developed a vision for the "big picture" of schools. She respected the authority of positions within the hierarchy. She respected power as it related to position.

Mattie was ambitious. She was charismatic. She was visionary. She was caring. And she wanted the power associated with the capacity of principal to ensure the development of her vision.

Mattie had a vision for the school. She hoped for the day that students, faculty, and community members would be proud to be associated with DHS. She also envisioned the school as an integral part of the neighborhood community. Her dream depicted Division contributing to the social and economic welfare of the community through better education of its students; by opening its doors to people within the neighborhood, making it truly a community school; and by seeking parental advice for, and participation in, their children's education.

I believe that Mattie did not see power and caring as dichotomous; that early understanding was mine. She saw them as concepts working together to enable the realization of a vision that would empower black students and, ultimately, the black community. Through various interviews, she indicated that teachers did not understand the necessity for high expectations of themselves and students; that she had to find ways to convince them of the need for excellence. She talked about her responsibility to *make* them understand, implying the use of power.

Mattie also understood the bureaucracy as necessary for order and justice to predominate. Her thrust was to be a leader/principal who had vision to see the big picture, to ensure that faculty ideas fit into the big picture, and to manage the school efficiently and effectively. Her stance was that until the district changed its organization, she would not give up any power that would endanger the school's or her position in the district.

At the risk of forcing an interpretation of power on Mattie, I would propose that Mattie's discussions of caring and power and her ensuing actions could be described as pursuing a liberational ethic of caring. She used her power to attempt to empower black students and the black community.

The following chapters look at the staff and how they reacted to caring and power; how they cared for each other; how they enacted power over their peers; and how they responded to Mattie's caring and power.

CHAPTER 6

The Staff: Wary and In Need of Care

Freedom shows itself or comes into being when individuals come together in a particular way, when they are authentically present to one another (without masks, pretenses, badges of office), when they have a project they can mutually pursue. . . . There must be a coming together of those who choose themselves as affected and involved. There must be an opening of a space between them . . . deeper and more significant than merely practical or worldly interests.
—Maxine Greene, *The Dialectic of Freedom,* 1988

The faculty at Division High was experienced, graying, and "reform-smart." Most had been in the district long enough to have seen school reforms come and go, and cycle again. With each "new" change, there was a predictable mixture of mild excitement, cynicism, and apathy. The year Mattie became principal, however, was different. The faculty, as a whole, allowed themselves to hope. They saw opportunities for a coming together of staff, administration, student body, and community to effect changes at DHS that were "deeper and more significant" than simply another educational reform.

In Mattie Johnson, they anticipated a leader who would establish an environment that would be conducive to building trust among the various groups throughout the school, who would work *with* the staff to ensure the success of site-based management and shared decision-making, and who held academic excellence for students as a primary goal. Above all, the staff members wanted to see in Mattie the person who would care enough about them that she would, as a faculty member suggested, "take risks." In other words, she would stand up to "downtown" in order to support her faculty and staff to do what was best for Division High School. The staff anticipated making changes, with Mattie's leadership, that would foster caring among themselves and a positive working relationship between staff and administration.

The atmosphere at DHS seemed ripe for the development of an ethic of caring. Mattie saw, and felt, the staff's need for nurturing and support. She embraced her role as the "one-caring" (Noddings, 1984) as a basic tenet of her conception of leadership; she would care for them. The staff was aware of their need for care, although the depth of that awareness varied among them. They sought her guidance in directing change that would lead to trust. Trust, in turn, would serve as the basis for cooperation and collaboration between them and administrators, and ultimately for their own empowerment. But, were they and Mattie, as she would say, "singin' from the same hymn book"?

From Noddings's (1984) perspective, relation is the ontological basis for caring and "the caring relation is ethically basic" (p. 3). Within the caring relationship is a set of ordered pairs: the one caring and the cared-for. In order for caring to exist, the development of reciprocity between the one caring and the cared-for must occur. That is, for the parties to care and to be cared for, each must contribute to the relation. The one caring, in some way, will feel completed in the cared-for if the relationship is depicted as caring. The cared-for is not simply a vessel to *receive* caring, but must be willing to acknowledge the caring act as such, reciprocating caring in return.

Additionally, the one caring, at times, may willingly suspend justice. She may defer the adherence to rules and regulations designed to ensure fairness via objectively judging a situation by criteria applied to all like situations. To see each circumstance as unique and, therefore, not bound by compliance to a set of regulations or directives is the aim of the one caring.

This and the subsequent two chapters focus on the staff, particularly on the ways in which their past and current experiences influence their abilities to give and receive care. Among the questions addressed are the following:

1. How do the staff members understand and interpret caring for themselves?

2. Is there reciprocity in terms of caring among themselves and between them and Mattie?

3. Do staff members view receiving and giving care as gaining power, that is, becoming empowered?

4. Is power/empowerment a necessary factor of an ethic of caring, or do caring and being cared for become subsumed in power-as-control?

I examine the staff, through their voices and through my observations and interpretations, in several ways. First, I consider the staff from the perspective of one body, that is, from the common perspectives they hold about the understandings, interpretations, and need for caring. In Chapter 7, I provide a detailed study of two groups within the staff. The first group is the most senior staff, who were a part of the evolution of DHS, now on the brink of retirement, and who experienced the conflicts and complications of desegregation, many of them at DHS, in Newtown. The second group comprises the members of the steering committee for site-based management. They held formal leadership roles to effect change at the school. Each of those groups represented important aspects of, and had significant impact on, the faculty as a whole. Chapter 8 highlights the perceptions of caring within the relationship between Mattie and a team of teachers who focused on a project to decrease the dropout rate at DHS. In each of those chapters, I probe for the staff's understandings and interpretations concerning their specific and, perhaps, different needs for caring. Chapters 7 and 8 are important, from a poststructuralist, feminist stance, to recognize that differences within and among the whole are critical to understanding the whole, that is, the staff.

IN NEED OF CARING

Common themes and issues surfaced among the general staff concerningtheir need for caring. Two main themes in virtually all faculty conversation were (1) the lack of trust within the staff, and between staff and administrators; and (2) the difficulty of caring for students.

Lack of Trust

Staff members interviewed evidenced, either directly or indirectly, the lack of trust within their ranks. They suggested that distrust among them limited the ways in which they did or did not collaborate as professionals, and restricted their personal interactions. Fragmentation of the staff, a result of unfriendliness, extreme individualism, and poor communication among themselves and between them and administration, was rudimentary to their inability to trust one another.

Fragmentation. The reality of a severely fragmented staff appeared to result in even greater isolation than Lortie (1975) and Jackson (1986) identify as problematic for teachers, for isolation extended beyond the classroom. Identifying social groups among the faculty was difficult. Few people made attempts to construct relationships, personal or professional, and rarely did the latter occur without mandates. A younger teacher who graduated from DHS commented on the lack of familiarity of teachers with one another.

> Generally, people have to really *seek* [teacher's emphasis] their cliques. It's hard to know who hangs with who[m]. I usually eat lunch in my room, or sometimes with [another teacher]. I don't even know who eats together, let alone who socializes with whom. I don't think many people at [Division] get together personally. We just work here. And we need to do more than that. That's why we don't work together— we don't know one another so we don't trust one another.

A teacher who had taught in several schools within the Newtown system for over 25 years noted particular relationships based on length of time at DHS and by shared discipline. Yet, her general assessment was that DHS was one of the "loneliest places" she's ever worked.

> There is a group that . . . I would call the original group . . . that has been here a long time. They seem to form a clique. . . . I think the math department is a very tight clique and very supportive of each other. Probably the tightest clique in the building. I think some of the people in the science department are, and then some are just not a part of that at all. That's another clique. . . . But, there is no central meeting place. . . . I don't really spend time with a lot of people in the building. . . . And I would say that's pretty much the [same for most] of the group here. . . . I try to keep . . . the relationships professional. . . . This was the first high school I'd been in. And, I've found it one of the loneliest experiences of my life . . . and I've been here 13 years.

Although that teacher noted there was no "central meeting place," there were two faculty lounges. Both, however, informally were designated as "belonging" to certain groups of teachers during particular periods of the school day.

Other teachers noted the lack of friendliness among the staff, attributing it to the size of the building and to a lingering reaction to the desegregation process. They perceived the lack of friendliness as precluding the staff's working well together.

> This school has never [had] a real friendly staff. From the time we started, I think people were too separated; we never see anybody. . . . You can teach for a whole year but the person that's on the other side of the building, you don't even know. . . . And it's always been like that here. [Before desegregation] we had a 6-hour day . . . [and] almost all the teachers ate during [a given] period. And you saw more people. Then . . . after the riots, we had a 5-hour day, and all the kids went home. Everybody had sixth-hour planning and we ate in our rooms because they didn't serve any lunches . . . you saw very few people. And I don't think teachers have ever totally bounced back.

Fragmentation resulted from the staff's individualism. Some teachers did not to want to identify with a group personally or professionally.

> We're a very fragmented staff. . . . It's just a very unique setup. . . . I feel like a loner, and I'd like to stay that way. I don't want to be a part . . . of a particular group. . . . And, [the faculty is] just that way here.

Some viewed the need for change at Division from only one perspective—
their particular one.

> People . . . [in this building] are so quick to judge. And they are so
> quick to say . . . somebody's a sell-out. . . . And it's not based on any-
> thing but what you want—"Well, *I* think it should be happening this
> way." Well, that's one *I* in the building of one hundred. What does ev-
> erybody else want?

Individualism, manifested in various pockets throughout the school, served
to maintain a staff that was splintered in its relationships to one another, and
increased the struggles for power among themselves. Proposals for new projects
engendered cynicism, for colleagues too often assumed fundamental self-interest
as the driving force behind the "innovation."

Not only did they have difficulty envisioning the "big picture," but
teachers resisted working together. To illustrate the problem, the head of one
of the larger school committees described the ways in which peers usually
carried out committee leadership. Staff members volunteered for leadership
positions, then circumvented procedures that faculty members themselves established for working with the appointed or elected committee to accomplish
a given task. The leader conceived what needed to be done and, through
informal contacts, checked with others who may or may not have been on
the formal committee. Decisions were made and actions carried out, often
without the knowledge of other committee members and without the consensus of the faculty as a whole. Not infrequently, individual staff members made
unilateral decisions, causing others to perceive that they were made in light
of particular people's needs rather than those of the faculty or entire school.
The result was an inability of faculty members to suspend distrust of their
colleagues to collaborate on projects that "fit" together to arrive at a unified
vision for Division High. "Decisions are made in a vacuum. People are thinking
about their own classes rather than everything that occurs in the building; they
don't want to compromise."

Efforts of the lead teacher in an academy[9] that was in the initial stages of
implementation illustrate such unilateral decision-making. Students were pulled
from other classes to fill the academy's classes and transported to work sites
outside the school without following legal protocol. Teachers who were not
a part of the program did not know that students would miss their classes for
academy internships. The teacher in question focused entirely on building the
program, neglecting to consider the effects his decisions had on the rest of the
staff. The result was that other teachers resisted active support for *any* academy.

Inadequate Communication. Faculty members stated that insufficient and inadequate communication was a serious problem, especially between administration and faculty. Teachers too often learned about incidences, students, or policies at DHS through the Newtown newspaper or from students. The main source of information in the school was daily announcements over the P.A. Several teachers indicated that this was not satisfactory because sound transmission was not clear and the noise level from student talking limited or prevented people from hearing the bulletins. The results were rumors leading to more mistrust.

When teachers did not have necessary information, they often were excluded from decision-making. A sense of frustration and isolation resulted, and, more important, there was a sense of *exclusion* from decisions. The latter intensified the lack of trust, fragmenting and isolating staff members further, and encouraging them to recall the "good old days" with a fondness that never really existed. A teacher who took an active role in school committees evidenced her frustration with the amount of effort she needed to expend in order to remain in the communication "loop."

> Until 3 or 4 years ago, everything was in writing. . . . I have felt this year that I have less information available to me than I'd ever had before [regarding my] knowing what's going on and when it's going on and if I'm supposed to be someplace at a certain time. . . . Often I'm forgotten because I'm back in the corner and it's easy to forget me back there. There is no good communication system.

Lack of a "good communication system" was a major contributor to the maintenance of the historically adversarial relations between administration and staff. Staff became bitter and even more distrustful of administrators. The result was that faculty expended even less effort to cooperate and collaborate in decision-making.

At the beginning of the year, staff members hoped that the new administrative team would make an effort to build trust at all levels in the building. By the end of the year, they felt that there was less exchange of information than in previous years. Teachers heard about decisions after they were made, and received little or no explanation about why a particular tack was taken. Administrators asked teachers for input on decisions, then appeared not to use it, resulting in teachers feeling used and patronized. The principal promised more individual communication with teachers, but the staff felt that less occurred than in previous years. Those feelings lead to bitterness and less trust between the two groups. One teacher's assessment of the issue seemed to incorporate the essence of many faculty comments.

I think that a lack of trust amongst us has been a problem for a long time and I don't think it's any better than it's ever been. A good part of that is due to a lack of communication. In my opinion, it is extremely important to make sure that everyone knows what's going on, to make sure that whenever possible, decisions are made by the group because then people buy into them. When a decision has to be made and it cannot be made by the group, either because it must be done in an emergency situation or because it's one of those things that fall strictly under the realm of administration, I think it's very important to let the staff know that the decision was made, why it was made, and why it could not be a joint decision-making effort. I think it's also very important to make sure that everyone knows what's going on in the building. Those things, in my opinion, are not happening. . . . Plus, decisions are made and sometimes I think there's a very legitimate reason for making those decisions, but because no one knows why they were made, it makes it very easy for mistrust to continue, because there's already a problem with mistrust in the building.

Not knowing the reasoning behind Mattie's decisions negatively contributed to teachers' perceptions of their relationships with her. They quickly—and comfortably?—returned to their long-held belief that administrators don't care about them. They disbelieved the rhetoric about collaboration, contending that Mattie determined *which* decisions were made jointly with teachers, and which she made unilaterally, all with no explanation.

An example of misunderstanding that developed because Mattie did not communicate her rationale behind a decision involved her limiting the time she spent walking the halls. As Mattie began to integrate her personal goals with those of the community, district, staff, and students, her workload took a different shape from that of the initial weeks she was in her position. She found herself dealing with paperwork; district, community, and university committees; individual conferences; and unplanned happenings, all of which required more time than she anticipated. As a new principal, she was not yet fully aware of which duties imposed by the district office she could delegate, negotiate, or dismiss entirely. The consequence was that she noticeably restricted the amount of time she spent in the hallways as a visible presence to staff and students. Mattie, moreover, did not explain to the staff why they no longer saw her as frequently in the halls between classes or stopping by their classrooms for a moment of two of conversation. Perhaps she assumed they understood. However, they clung to her initial promise that she would be visible and available to them. Observing her less in the halls, they surmised that they, again, had been duped. Mattie's failure to communicate her dilemmas to faculty put both her and them in positions of feeling not cared for. A teacher, supportive of the principal, noted, "If she's involved in other things that she can't get out of, I want her to tell me what those are and why she can't get out of them, even though I know she's not obligated to do that. I would feel less frustrated, and I think that's what I'm talking about by communication."

Communication meant much more than conveying information or giving encouragement and support. The teacher quoted above asked for caring that required Mattie to trust her. Although Mattie was not obligated to disclose the reasoning behind her decisions, doing so would have shown caring to the teacher; it would have evidenced trust. By trusting her, Mattie also would have opened the door to a reciprocal relation of caring that I believe is even more encompassing than that which Noddings insists is critical to an ethic of caring: Mattie would have allowed herself to be the cared-for by the teacher, who would have assumed the role of the one caring.[10]

Lack of trust, generally, permeated DHS. Some teachers attributed it to an extremely fragmented staff. An inadequate communication system, limiting and often preventing staff members' receipt of information, also contributed to a growing distrust, leaving many people feeling isolated, inadequate, and powerless.

Staff members not only grappled with the latter in their relationships among themselves and with administrators, but with their connections to students.

To Care for Students

Staff members needed caring themselves in order to care for students. Professionally, many teachers felt pressure from the community and from school reforms to improve student learning. Yet, when they tried to improve student learning and achievement, they received little or no support from colleagues and administrators for their efforts or, worse, they were criticized and stymied in their attempts.

Personally, staff members struggled with the trauma and violence of many of their students' lives. They recognized that each time a student was hurt or killed, their own lives were affected. As they discussed their relationships with students, the magnitude of the effects of the relationships between students and teachers was clear. Yet, few teachers chose to speak directly about those relationships.

In this section, I examine teachers' perceptions of their relationships and responsibilities to students and the way students' lives affect teachers and what they do in schools.

High Expectations for Students. Teachers experienced frustration in their efforts to care for students regarding expectations for student achievement and learning. There seemed to be general agreement among the administration and staff that expectations and standards for students were not high enough. Yet, individual teachers or groups of teachers who attempted to ameliorate that situation seemingly did not receive the support needed. Teachers who tried to develop a school-within-a-school or implement ninth-grade team concepts felt unsupported and uncared-for by their peers and the principal regarding the most important aspect of teaching: the continual pursuit of better ways to teach and learn.

Members of the mathematics department supported one another in their setting and maintenance of high standards for all students taking math, regardless of level. They, however, did not believe other staff members and administrators supported them in their expectations for high student achievement. In fact, they seemed to feel that administrators attempted to dissuade them by pressuring them to pass students who attended regularly and did not cause trouble, and that counselors discarded their standards by placing students in classes the math teachers indicated were inappropriate for particular students. Although supported by their own department members, the math faculty regularly was the recipient of snide comments—"Who do they think they are, holding such high standards?" "Do they think they're better than other departments?" "They can't tell us what classes to put these kids in"—from other teachers and from counselors. The result was that the math faculty formed a tight bond among themselves and a we-against-the-rest-of-the-school attitude.

Student Attendance

Teachers were frustrated by high student absenteeism. At the same time that they talked about raising standards, they agonized over ways to keep children coming to school, and resented the criticism they received because students seemed not to learn even the "basics." A social studies teacher showed me the daily absent sheet for DHS: 176 ninth graders; 65 tenth graders; 33 eleventh graders; and 30 twelfth graders were absent on one day. On that same day in his ninth-grade classes alone, there were 14 absences out of 35 students registered for first hour; 16 out of 31 for second hour; and 10 out of 33 for third hour. He commented laconically, "If students are not here, you don't have any bodies, you can't teach. You can't teach without bodies."

When asked about the failure rate in his classes due to absenteeism, his reply was sardonic, yet matter-of-fact: "The school board has a ruling that I may fail students after 15 days [of absenteeism in one semester] if the work is not made up. But, we kind of bend the rules here. . . . As long as [a student] does half the work . . . or a little more, [he pauses]. This is what we talk about, lowering standards."

Ironically, although teachers were distressed by students' lack of regular attendance, they bemoaned the new assistant principal's reluctance to suspend students from school. Some of the faculty felt that he evidenced nonsupport for staff by allowing students to remain in school after they had been sent to the discipline office. A counselor compared him with his predecessor, newly promoted to the position of deputy principal at DHS, who was "strong and dished out punishments and suspensions to keep the kids in line. [The new assistant principal] is a fool. He's not doing his job on discipline." Some faculty resented his sending the students back to their classrooms, reasoning that if they could have dealt with them in the first place, they would not have demanded they leave.

To better manage the discipline situation, the steering committee of SBM appointed a committee to investigate ways of keeping students in school. The committee recommended in-school suspension, which required hiring someone to monitor those students. Adding to the staff was unacceptable, for the school board stipulated that teachers could do anything within SBM as long as it did not cost money. The committee presented an alternative plan that increased each teacher's class size by two students so that one teacher would be free each hour to monitor the in-school suspension room. There were so many complaints from teachers that the proposal did not even reach the steering committee's agenda. Yet, teachers generally were most upset about the lack of support for the committee's recommendations. Their interpretation of support, however, referred to the board's adamant stance against expending money for another hire; few staff members referred to the alternative proposal. There seemed to be questions of whether staff really cared about students and, if so, how much.

Teachers battled a sense of futility as they attempted to keep kids in school and raise academic expectations for students and standards for student achievement, while simultaneously running into roadblocks from colleagues and administrators. The teachers, by and large, did care about their students in various ways and to different degrees. But for each attempt they made at caring, I believe they expended as much energy *fighting for the right to care*.

Students' Personal Lives

Conversely, teachers sought to maintain distance between themselves and students in order to protect themselves, not from violent acts, but from caring too much. As in Kotlowitz's book *There Are No Children Here* (1991), trauma and violence were part of the everyday lives of many students at DHS. The effects and residuals of those aspects became part of the teachers' lives. Although many teachers tried to remain "objective" and aloof from the almost routine traumatic events that involved their students, most found doing so impossible. Teachers regularly learned about current or former students who managed difficult domestic situations daily; who were involved in crimes often associated with drug dealing; who were physically or sexually assaulted by relatives or friends; who were severely beaten in gang fights; or who were violently killed.

Domestic Difficulties. Almost daily, teachers heard of students who moved from one household to another, who were pregnant, whose parent lost a job, or who left home with no place to go. As a participant in the university partnership with DHS, I taught a class of ninth graders for 6 weeks. Through writing assignments and casual conversations, I learned that four of the girls in the class had borne children and two had two babies. Only one of the girls, with the help of her parents, kept her baby. She told me that she wanted to write a book about her experience as a black teenage mother to dispel the notion that black teenage girls are "no good" and that they "would get a good education even if they did have a baby."

I vowed to help her at least begin to write that book. We never even got started because she did not return to class after we had that conversation. When I spoke to the teacher with whom I was working, his response was to tell me he did not know she had a child and he did not know much about the students in his classes unless he had to. He reasoned that he had enough problems of his own and could not take on the students' problems, too. Besides, he could not help them anyway. There was frustration and anger in his voice when he blurted out that, yes, maybe he should learn more about the students, but he just couldn't afford to!

During a planning period, a teacher regaled me and several teachers with stories about students' fantastic excuses for being absent. As he was about to leave, he became somber, saying he had one more.

A ninth-grade girl had been absent for several days. When the teacher questioned other students about her absence, no one seemed to know why she was not in school. A few days later as he was walking down the hall, he heard a student call him. He turned around to see the girl whom he had missed in his class. She approached him and began to explain why she had been absent. She had been in the hospital, she said. He was about to ask her why when she pulled out a glossy photograph from a manila envelope and thrust it in his face. As he adjusted his focus to determine what the picture was, the girl told him she had an abortion; the picture was of the aborted fetus.

Before the teacher could think of something to say, the student grabbed the picture, stuffed it back into the envelope, smiled, and said she'd see him in class. She left him—"standing with my mouth open"—as she almost bounced away, calling to a friend and waving the envelope.

The incident occurred several years earlier, but remained vivid in his mind. He looked at us, particularly at me, and said that he's pretty tough, but "this really got to me. I still can't forget it. Yah, these kids really go through some rough things." This big, burly man slowly got up from his chair, shaking his head as if trying to rid himself of the image in his memory, and walked out of the lounge, leaving the rest of us in silence.

In both instances, the teachers were not unaffected by their students' personal lives. But both chose to stuff away, as best they could, those aspects of the students they felt they could do nothing about. They were at DHS to teach, which they chose to understand as academics.

Violence and Crime. Teachers hear about robberies, drug dealings, and gang fights through the news media and immediately speculate about whether or not those named are or were students at DHS. One day as I was working in the library's media center, a teacher rushed in obviously agitated. A student had told her that another DHS student had been shot trying to rob a crackhouse. The teacher was looking for the morning paper to verify the story. She said the student in question was one she had taught the year before and, if the story was true, that would make five DHS students shot during the school year to date. She followed with the comment that she hated to turn on the TV or radio, or read the newspaper, because she feared hearing about more students hurt or killed.

Several teachers talked about the four student murders during the year. Each of their conversations with me usually would end in a shrug and a question like, "Well, what can we do?" One teacher captured the essence of teachers' attempts to simply absorb the violent and traumatic events in students' lives when she said, "You get too depressed looking into the problems because every time you hear someone at this end of town gets hurt, you wonder, 'Is that another one of ours?' It doesn't make it easy."

Defending DHS. Finally, because of the violence that occurred to and among Division students, teachers often felt they had to expend too much energy defending themselves for teaching at DHS, and defending DHS students to the public. A teacher strongly made the point that "you're not constantly thinking of weapons, and who's out to get you, things like that. I mean I'm not scared to walk in this building . . . yet with the general public you have to rationalize where you are; you have to be defensive."

The attitude of the community, in essence, added pressure to the teachers' relationships with their students. The teachers felt the negative attitude of community members toward Division High—its students and faculty. The result, according to a teacher who has been at the school for 25 years, was:

> I tend to defend [the students] . . . even sometimes maybe more than I
> need to . . . with outsiders. . . . [I] try to push [the students] so it makes

them look better outside, because if you see them out on the streets and when they're doing something dumb, you wish they wouldn't.

Regardless of the teachers' conscious decisions concerning the level of their involvement in students' personal lives, no teacher was left unaffected. Some developed "hard shells so we don't have to feel"; others felt, but often wished they did not. All, however, were frustrated and angry because they seemed to feel alone in their struggles and unable to make headway.

The struggle to work and relate to students seemed to correlate significantly with the lack of trust within the DHS staff. The atmosphere of mistrust at Division created and maintained a fragmented staff; it also limited or prevented what teachers could do with and for students.

> I don't think there's been a great deal of real honesty that has gone on for a long time. And that's part of what breaks down communication, and that's part of what causes mistrust. . . . You take things out on the people who can't fight back and, you know, [that's the kids]. . . . Certainly if you are frustrated and you feel unhappy, and you feel that other people perceive you as not doing a good job, we're like everybody else; it's that self-fulfilling prophecy. We live up to people's expectations of us. . . . And when you feel that you are not trusted, and you feel that you are not seen as doing a good job, you tend to look at other people, students, the same way.

CHAPTER 7

The Staff as Unique Groups

The word "change" . . . has been given a new meaning: it no longer means a new
stage of coherent development *(as it was understood by Vico, Hegel, and Marx),
but a* shift from one side to another, *from front to back, from the back to the left,
from the left to the front.*

—Milan Kundera, *Immortality*, 1990 [emphasis in original]

In Chapter 6, I considered the staff as one body needing and struggling to
find caring. In light of poststructural, feminist theory, however, I must locate
the various groups within that body as they individually and collectively view
their need for caring in order to understand the individuals that compose the
whole. Poststructuralist feminisms "ground their epistemology on the foundation of difference," making "conceptual space for difference in subject location,
identity and knowledges" (Luke & Gore, 1992, p. 7). In terms of this study,
the concept of difference takes into consideration the notion that although
there are some common issues for the whole staff, they are not definitive
issues that represent the interests of *all* individuals and groups within the
whole. Therefore, in this and the following chapter, I discuss unique groups
that affect the identity of the collective staff.

Among Division's faculty were many groups that contributed in interesting
ways to the functioning of the staff. I chose to explore three, each of which
had a significant impact on the faculty and administration as they pursued
change and reform efforts at Division High. Each of the groups, in its own
manner, sought to care; each also greatly needed to receive care.

The senior members of the faculty constitute one group. Those teachers
had been in the Newtown school system for 20 or more years. They were
older, more cynical, and more tired than the new staff. They carried a shared
history with them that influenced their day-to-day teaching and the way they
viewed the future. They constituted almost half of the faculty and, therefore,
greatly influenced the changes that occurred, or did not occur, at Division.

Another major group was the faculty on the steering committee, the governance body of site-based management. Their peers elected them to implement
site-based management, a system of organization no one really understood;

95

consequently, their roles were not clear. Although they functioned within an ambiguous situation, attempting to clarify roles and procedures that would create an atmosphere of collaboration and empowerment for faculty, teachers and administrators criticized their efforts as increasing the fragmentation and mistrust already prevailing in the staff.

In Chapter 8, I examine the third group, the ninth-grade team members, whom I call the teacher innovators. Because they tried to develop and effect major projects that required changing not only pedagogy and classroom practices, but also school organization, they needed the collaboration of a variety of groups involved with DHS. They needed cooperation from fellow teachers, from administrators, from the community business committee, and from the university representatives. They also needed collaboration to occur among and between those groups. The teacher innovators found themselves often caught in the middle of unspoken power struggles as they sought collaboration.

Within those groups of teachers, I examine the relationships among the members as they labor to care for themselves and to understand caring from Mattie's perspective. I also explore the relationships between Mattie and the individual groups as they affected her attempts to establish a caring community. Two major questions concerning the reciprocity of caring evolved from the study of the three groups:

1. Is it possible for caring and power to be so integrated that there is difficulty in producing the reciprocal relationship Noddings indicates is necessary for an ethic of care to exist?
2. Conversely, is power needed in order to produce caring relationships that are reciprocal?

With these questions in mind, I begin with the senior staff members whose present continued to reflect the past.

SENIOR STAFF MEMBERS: WARY AND WEARY

As was typical in the Newtown school district, the staff members at Division High were older. Many began their teaching careers in the district and stayed for the next 20 to 30 years. They participated in numerous educational reforms and in a variety of university-initiated projects at their respective schools. Virtually all of them experienced desegregation of the city's schools and, personally and professionally, felt the impact of that process. They saw the city grow and prosper and, at the time of the study, witnessed its rapid decline and fight for survival. Finally, they apprehended their own growth, rise, and decline. They began to face aging bodies and souls, and the resultant problems and dilemmas that often accompany such seasoning—personal and/or a partner's illnesses; death of parents; reduced energy; approaching retirement; and increased skepticism and cynicism about education particularly and about the world generally.

Their longevity in the district and particularly at DHS had an effect on the senior staff members that was almost incomprehensible to relative newcomers at the school. Because of their extensive histories as Newtown educators, some of the senior constituents reflected on their needs for caring that required an understanding different from that sought by their less experienced colleagues. Many seemed weary of trying to teach adolescents who came with troubled backgrounds and little hope for the future. But many also were wary of one another as a result of the history they helped create, and that tore them apart from each other. Divisions between teachers deepened because of the past, as evidenced in the following comment: "There's so much meanness and resentment. I mean there's things that go way deep here, and as one person's involved, there're five others that won't be just because of the dynamics of previous experiences." The years of desegregation were responsible for many of the previous experiences that went "way deep," and created and maintained the dynamics that led to a wariness and alienation among senior staff members.

Veterans of Desegregation

The decision of Newtown's citizens[11] in the late 1960s to voluntarily desegregate their high schools had a lasting effect on the teachers and staff members who lived through the process and were teaching at DHS during the 1990s. Even though school desegregation resulted from a city-wide election, and thus was "voluntary," the actual process of increasing the black student population at Division was not without opposition and incident.[12]

As mentioned earlier, Newtown citizens considered DHS the "country club" school when it was built in the middle 1960s. With the desegregation process, however, its reputation hit bottom and had yet to recover at the time of this study. People with any personal ties to Newtown reacted negatively to the mention of Division High School. Virtually all DHS teachers were sensitive to its reputation as the worst school in Newtown, but those teachers who lived through all or part of the desegregation process continued to live with the anguish of the past.

What did that pain look like? It was not blatant or worn as a badge. It was something that undergirded people's thoughts and actions, something that was supposed to be buried. On occasion, however, the pain refused to stay hidden and surfaced to open old wounds people believed were healed over with thick scars. Talking about the 1960s was not easy for those teachers. An automatic response when broaching the topic of "the past" was to rise from one's chair, close the door, and lower one's voice, for that era pivoted on one event: desegregation. Their thoughts of that period summoned images of police inside and outside the building, students fighting students, teachers fighting teachers, students fighting teachers: racial tension and violence. Massive distrust among and between teachers, administrators, and students, white and black, conservative and liberal, ensued. As one teacher commented, "You didn't *really* trust your best friend."

A continuing sense of wariness seemed to stalk those who lived through the attempts to integrate schools. As teachers recalled that period, their faces showed strain and their eyes looked haunted. In their reticence to discuss, and in the caution used when discussing, those racial incidents, I sensed the teachers' present distrust of current colleagues as an extension of past uneasiness with racial relations. Consider the following exchange emanating from a conversation about efforts to desegregate.

Responding to a question about stress between the races at DHS during attempts to integrate, a teacher noted that the racial tension "back then was awful. You were afraid to say anything to anybody. You couldn't trust your best friend." When asked about tension between white and black teachers in the present, the teacher responded there were no such problems among faculty. However, later in the conversation the person indicated that several "black staff members are getting involved with things [becoming heads of committees] and can't cope with the power." What did the latter mean? The interpretation was that a black teacher who had become a committee head went from being a "nice, friendly person to being obnoxious," seemingly because the teacher attempted to make other faculty members take responsibility for follow-through on a project they had voted to accept.

In another instance, white teachers who had been at Division during the desegregation process resented a black teacher's seeking and accepting advice in order to become a more effective committee chairperson. Negative comments concerning the teacher's ambitions beyond classroom teaching abounded, often prefaced with, "Who does [she] think she is anyway, the next black principal?"

Another teacher commented on social relationships within faculty and the rarity of interracial groups. As an African American, she also noted her feeling of "invisibility" in a school that is 99% black. Additionally, she questioned the degree to which African American teachers influenced policy for the students at DHS.

> As a matter of fact, I didn't realize there was this many black [teachers]
> until I sat down one day to count because so many times I feel invisi-
> ble. And, I mean, not me per se, because I get around and talk to ev-
> erybody, but as a member of a group I felt that the group was invisi-
> ble. You know, I actually had to sit down and say, "Okay, now who's

here?" in order to realize that half our staff is black. . . . It's a strange
kind of feeling when you not only look at people who are existing in
the building as being invisible, but at the reality of it, too. . . . You're
looking at a school that has this very high percentage of black students,
and who do you think will be looking at the policies to truly impact
black students? . . . Why is it that we as black people, understanding all
of the obstacles for young people who don't have an education, why
aren't we . . . making policies for this school?

Although not the sole reason for the distrust at Division, racial tensions
contributed to the wariness among faculty. Variations in positions of power
often bring discomfort and apprehension among those affected by the changes.
Jealousy, resentment, or a "prove-yourself" attitude is not uncommon when
new people take over. At DHS, not only was Mattie in that position as a new
principal, but black teachers who began to volunteer for and be elected to
important committee leadership positions also were. Underlying the expected
skepticism and wariness associated with change, however, was a lingering sense
of fear, distrust, and perhaps anger among white teachers who saw and felt
the imposition of black students and teachers on DHS nearly 20 years earlier.
As the position changes took place, the veteran white teachers noted not only
those changes, but that the positions were filled by *black* staff members. That
is, lack of trust and uncertainty stemmed not only from doubt concerning the
person's capability to perform in a leadership role, but from the knowledge
that the person was *black*.

There was discontent among several white teachers, particularly males,
who had sought administrative posts but had not been selected. They hinted
that they had been passed over in favor of black applicants. Although unspoken,
those thoughts sustained the atmosphere of distrust between white and black
teachers and administrators.

Mistrust further grew as a result of the tenure of the previous black
principal. His style was gentle and caring, and he spent much of his time and
energy interacting with students and faculty. Faculty did not consider him
dynamic, for he made few, if any, major educational changes, and seemed
content with establishing and maintaining relationships. Many teachers appreciated the relationships he fostered, valuing the calm after years of racial strife
and tension. Yet, the staff did not view him as a "strong" leader, for he did
little to alter the poor reputation of DHS within the school district and community. Because of that, some saw him as lazy, even incompetent. A younger
black teacher interpreted the effect the principal had on the faculty.

I think it did not help that we had a black male principal that was laid
back. I think that for a black man to be in control of a building, he has

to be viewed as being in control and brooking no nonsense. And not to the point that he's uncaring, but, just enough that you know who your principal is and you know where he's going to stand.

She, as well as other teachers, associated his "weak" leadership with his race. That is, because he was "laid back," he was an incompetent *black* principal, rather than simply an incompetent principal. That notion exacerbated the unspoken—and unacknowledged—racial tensions. There was an undercurrent of anger among white teachers for their having to suffer for the lack of leadership ability of a black leader appointed, no doubt, to fulfill affirmative action requirements. Concurrently, black teachers experienced anger because a "brother" did not live up to their expectations and consequently they felt in the position of having to defend him and to rationalize his nonaction because he was a "brother."

Mattie complicated the situation more because she was a black female. For many of the white, as well as black, males, she represented the strong-willed, controlling female, the Sapphire of the Amos and Andy shows who browbeat the men with her black female will. In the words of a black female, Mattie "came in as a strong, black woman. Well, there's a lot of stuff revolving around those 'black star sapphires' in your mind, and so the perception was a female, black, who would take no nonsense from anyone." White men had as hard or harder a time dealing with her. Not only was she a woman, but she was black. A counselor who began teaching at DHS when it opened, drew attention to the impact of race on the current staff.

I think that [Mattie's] being principal irritates the white, middle-aged men. They'd have a hard time with a woman, period, but with a *black* [emphasis hers] woman as principal . . . ! And to make matters worse, they have to deal with a *black* [emphasis hers] male deputy principal who we all feel is incompetent.

There appeared to be tacit agreement among the staff to refrain from speaking about racial issues and anything that might lead to such discussion among themselves. They were, in effect, denying the importance of race to the general lack of trust prevalent among the staff. Failing to address that in a school whose student body was 99% and whose staff was 50% black only perpetuated distrust by preventing open, honest communication. One of the members of the steering committee for SBM recognized the importance not only of communication among faculty, but, particularly, of communication allowing and encouraging them to face the underlying racism within the school.

[Racism] is what it comes back down to when I talk about those people relation skills. The people relation skills do need some work to show that caring, nurturing kind of sensation because racism is a very, very strong feeling, and people just don't know how or want to deal with it. . . . We need some real, I don't want to say confrontations, because I don't think people getting emotional and upset solves anything. But we need dialogue where people will listen and ponder and it will make you have to look at the things you say and do.

Her concern was that people, by not engaging in discourse, evaded confronting their own fears, anxieties, and biases regarding African American–European American race relationships. Lack of such communication surfaced in various ways, one of which was in the seating arrangement of faculty members at meetings, as pointed out by a senior staff person: "Did you notice how staff sits in staff meetings? Whites at one table and blacks at another. I think the racial split has gotten worse and worse." Failing to deal with those feelings damaged the potential for collaboration among teachers and between teachers and administrators, and ultimately hurt the association teachers had with students.

Mattie viewed building trust as a major priority necessary to establish a caring environment for the DHS community. She viewed personal communication with staff members, ministering to their personal needs, and having integrity as ways to build the foundation for trust between herself and them. Because of the history of Division, she needed also to consider ways of building trust *among* the staff. "Caring" appeared to require that Mattie recognize the lingering effects of desegregation on teachers who lived through the process, and the continued—or escalated—distrust among them as a result of unspoken and/ or denied racial tension. If ignored, veteran teachers' association of trauma with desegregation had the potential to sabotage Mattie's or others' efforts to develop trusting relationships among the racially diverse faculty.

Veterans of the District and of Division High

Change involving building trust, redesigning the governance structure of the school, and re-visioning the curriculum was a concern among faculty members generally. Those who had been at Division for many years, however, viewed those efforts from a different perspective. As Kundera (1990) described change, they, too, no longer viewed it as "a new stage of coherent development," but perceived it as using the old ideas, but simply shifting them "from one side to another, from front to back, from the back to the left, from the left to the front" (p. 116).

Lack of trust among the staff was not a new issue, but one that continued to recycle. There was a weariness as veteran teachers talked about past efforts to establish trust among themselves and to make changes generally. They

102   *School Leadership*

observed the current concern for change as just another round of activity that swelled with momentary interest and enthusiasm, and deflated as quickly. A teacher recalled attempts to build community years ago when she first began teaching at DHS.

> Well, we've been talking about getting along together, you know, the idea of the perception of trust and, everybody sharing decisions. . . . Anyway, that's been an ongoing thing. . . . I came here 14 years ago and we were talking about it then. . . . Well, we tried a little something and it didn't work. . . . For a while we didn't do anything, and then we tried again. The staff dinner, the staff potluck, this kind of stuff. We've done this repeatedly.

When probed to think about efforts to build trust that did not revolve around social situations, but that were directed to developing interdependence among staff members, the teacher replied that the staff was still not working together. The faculty member indicated, again, that she had been in the district and at DHS long enough to know that past efforts had failed and most likely the current efforts would also.

> I mean this is not suddenly this year we're going to get together, and work together. We've done this over the years. . . . Sometimes the [approach is the] same one, sometimes different, and ones with little variations. But . . . we didn't just discover the wheel this year.

Another veteran of the district pointed to the attempts to institute site-based management, which would provide for shared decision-making among staff and therefore would require the existence of at least a modicum of trust. She reflected on the current efforts in light of her past experiences at a different school with some of the same teachers with whom she now worked. Her comments represented an attitude toward change typical of teachers who had experienced and participated in numerous reforms over many years. There was a tiredness in her voice and a plea for understanding. Above all, there was an appeal for valuing what she *could* contribute and for not criticizing her for what she could not.

> The three of us taught in the high school together for 4 years. . . . We've done this, we've done site-based. . . . It worked, kind of. I don't want to do it again. I can't go through that again.

The teachers did not oppose the "new" attempts to build trust and to implement other changes. They wrestled, however, with their past experience of failed efforts, with the amount of energy required to accomplish the needed changes, and with their acquired knowledge of what worked and what did not. The past, ultimately, determined the degree to which they would involve themselves in current innovations and reorganization. Another round of reform seemed only to increase the weariness of teachers. Although they struggled not to "give up," they also were not prepared to abandon the methods with which, and the organization in which, they had learned to work.

> I'm getting also older. And I'd love to deal with how one sees problems [from different sides]. . . . I was criticized one time for being too conservative . . . but maybe I'm not afraid of that label anymore. I'm not ready to just tear down everything and start new.

As a newly appointed department head, a senior teacher received a request to serve on a committee to determine the process by which DHS would meet new state requirements for changes in school organization, curriculum, and student achievement and evaluation. Although viewed as "actively participating" in change by faculty members and administrators, she did not necessarily commit to the changes. She met expectations, but volunteered no more.

> I just don't concern myself a whole lot with policy unless it's something that really disturbs me. . . . I have a tendency to ignore what I don't want to deal with and shut the door and do my own classes. Forget about the rest. . . . I've been here a number of years and sometimes I've seen things—that policies that are for administrators . . . [the policies] aren't going to be here forever. So, if I stay out of the way, eventually things will get better. Which doesn't make me a real active person, but I guess it keeps me sane.

She was yet another teacher who found a way to work as a part of the school community and yet to remain apart. Hers was not so much a plea for understanding as a personal reconciliation with the effects that age, time, and numerous encounters with school reform left on her. She needed caring that entailed others' tolerance or acceptance of her resolve.

Finally, age and experience were major considerations—and at times major roadblocks—to innovation and educational reform. A younger teacher, committed to the academy concept, faced the reluctance of older staff to pledge the necessary time and effort that major curriculum changes required. Although many supported academies in theory, they hesitated to involve themselves because of past failures and because their workloads, again, would increase.

> [We're] trying to . . . just structure what [the academy] might look like. And then this summer we're going to work on curriculum in the biol-

ogy area. Now . . . with the number of our students that aren't successful, I thought that everybody in the building would be willing to sign
up for something like this. I'm the only one that's gone to every department and talked to them. . . . It was an eye-opening experience.
The staff is older. We've been through a lot of changes, we've seen
things come and go—and not work. And it's part of the problem—people are not so gung-ho on something like that because it's going to be
work. . . . [But] everybody [said], "Well, I hope this goes. I wish you
luck, but I don't want any part of it." The comments that I heard
were, "Well, show me a little bit more structure." "Do you have any
problems with this extra teacher?" "Do you have any money to make
this go?" And, of course, we have to say no, that nothing's in place.

Senior staff members were skeptical. They were wary of committing
themselves to projects that theoretically were sound, but, based on past history,
were ill-funded financially and lacked sufficient human resources. Age and
experience resulted in increased skepticism and a reluctance to expend energy
that was not as easily generated and renewed as it was 20 years before. As I
recall those teachers, I conceive a group of people who used their power to
protect themselves, thus caring for themselves.

A veteran teacher of almost 30 years spoke eloquently about the necessity
to recognize the position and place aging teachers had in any change process.
She described a need for caring that recognized the interest of older teachers
to be a part of the process, but realized they no longer wanted to shoulder
the efforts. Her thrust was that older teachers did not want to be discounted
because they chose—for a variety of reasons—to limit their involvement, but
wanted to be respected and valued for the experience they brought and for
what they *could* do.

In any situation you need to have older teachers because they are seasoned, they have experience, and they know how to handle some situations just because they have had experience. . . . The other side of it is,
you need young people. They bring in the enthusiasm, they are the
ones that really are . . . the change-makers. Because they're willing to
jump in, they don't know enough to know that everything's never going to work. So they're willing to jump in and they're willing to do everything and they bring along a lot of the folks with them. And I have
heard some of my colleagues say, "I'm old enough to jump on a bandwagon . . . I mean I can still jump on a bandwagon and I still would
like to see things change, but I'm too old to be the head cheerleader."
And I feel that way, too. . . . I have been on so many bandwagons and
have been a part of enough that I'm not sure if I'm ready [again] to do
what it would take.

Many older staff members desired to be valued and understood for their past accomplishments. They also wanted respect for their current contributions to DHS, and they did not want other staff, particularly those less experienced, demanding more of them than they could give.

In addition to educational changes, senior staff members faced aging and dealing with the effects, physically and emotionally, of growing old: They encountered more personal physical ailments and/or managed spouses and/or parents with physical problems; they dealt with the deaths of parents, siblings, or in-laws. In less than a year, one teacher had heart surgery, one died of a heart attack, two were out because of lengthy illnesses, one's spouse had major surgery, several had a parent or parent-in-law die, and one had two relatives murdered by a former student. Additionally, divorce severely disrupted several of the already-weary teachers. All those events—"normal" processes of life— only compounded the senior staff members' need for caring—the need to have their skepticism understood and to be accepted for what they were able to give to change.

SITE-BASED MANAGEMENT STEERING COMMITTEE MEMBERS: DEALING WITH AMBIGUITY

Unlike many of the senior staff, members of the steering committee (SC) wanted to believe SBM would bring a "new stage of coherent development" to Division. They intended to pave the way for collaboration and shared decision-making among and between all groups, thereby flattening the traditional hierarchical, authoritative model of organization. However, they had no model to follow as they embarked on change they hoped would be more than moving from front to back or side to side. They were unprepared for the personal toll of having to act within a field of ambiguity. The SC members needed caring as they dealt with abstruseness that was either unrecognized or unacknowledged by other teachers and administrators.

A deep sense of frustration penetrated the SC members as they attempted to understand and define their roles. Minutes of the SC exhibit the multiple perceptions of the committee's role and goals by both the staff and the members themselves. The SC held a meeting at the beginning of the year, bringing in a facilitator from the district office to help address the following:

DISCUSSION OF STEERING COMMITTEE SITUATION:
Some agreement that we lack effectiveness
Do we need a "retreat" in order to define ourselves?
Discussion centered on the need for a facilitator for such a
meeting

Role clarification—What are we supposed to do?
Why are we still talking about the process at this date?
A leading indicator is the absence of many members
Agreement that we would need to know the outcome that we
expect from such a meeting prior to holding it
Why is it that we aren't getting closure on our projects:
- Is it because we aren't communicating?
- Is it because we don't have the time to communicate?
- Is it because we have no source of money?
- Is it because the steering committee doesn't know what its
job is?

They found themselves striving for unity, yet exhibiting fragmentation, a quality they hoped SBM would diminish in the whole staff. Minutes of yet another SC meeting evidenced their continued struggle to define their role within the concept of SBM.

ROLE OF STEERING COMMITTEE MEMBERS: at Fishbowl
Meetings [whole staff meetings to discuss and vote on school policy, new school projects]
Problem: We have agreed to act as one and speak as one—we did not, conveying a message of fragmentation of the committee. A good deal of discussion took place about what it means when a proposal from this committee goes to the Fishbowl.

The SC members became a target of blame for generating a heightened sense of fragmentation and distrust among the staff. Teachers accused the committee of not "accomplishing things for kids," while the committee saw itself as the facilitator to enable faculty members to take responsibility for making changes that would lead to those accomplishments. In one instance, a faculty member attending a steering committee meeting leveled the following charges:

[Summary of comments made by teacher]
The steering committee needs credibility—by which he means accomplishing things for kids. He thinks the staff is fragmented, feels that the whole variety of projects underway produces more fragmentation, instead of being unified. He wants to see something completed—the site-based process isn't credible because we haven't completed anything. He wants colleagues to support each other. He feels completing a project will cause many who doubt our viability to join the process.

Although the teachers elected the members to the SC, and although the SC was vaguely understood to be the body that would assist teachers in gaining empowerment, a common perception among teachers was that the committee was only another layer of bureaucracy and not a part of *them*. The following comments from two teachers, one older and one younger, are only a small sample of the teachers who felt alientated from the process.

> Now when [we went] to site-based, I was . . . excited about it. But what I've seen over the year and a half, there's been a lot of meetings, . . . a lot of talk. Nothing gets done, but goes from the steering committee to another committee. [older teacher]

> You look at the steering committee and you see who persistently is there. It's an isolated group. . . . The rest of us in the building, really, have no perception of them as a part of us. [younger teacher]

The ambiguity associated with SBM fostered misunderstandings and misconceptions about the role of the SC. Teachers wanted the committee to carry out their wishes; administrators feared the committee would take their authority. Those attitudes affected the individual members of the committee in numerous ways. Members felt personally attacked, isolated, alienated, bitter, and ineffective.

The chairperson saw her role as leader, the one responsible for keeping the big picture in mind. She viewed her role as "investigative," that is, one in which she checked out the "hidden agendas" behind the information and proposals brought to the steering committee. She felt responsible for keeping the committee and faculty focused on "[Division's] overall vision," the "overall direction of the school and the school as part of the district, and the overall improvement of the school," as the committee considered initiatives from teachers for policies and projects.

To meet her responsibilities, she sought mentorship from the principal, whom she admired. Her goals were to conduct efficient meetings, to work effectively with people, to keep the big picture in mind, rather than becoming mired in detail or sidetracked in projects that did not contribute to the overall vision for the school. She desired to use her leadership position to represent the teachers to building and district administrators in the best ways possible. Rather than seeing her as a representative of the faculty and working for them, however, teachers and committee members often made comments that suggested she used her role to gain power.

> She's just a butt-licker, a clone of [Mattie]. Who does she think she is, the next black female principal? She rubs people the wrong way. We

can't get in to see [Mattie] because she's always in there. She's feeling power and doesn't know how to use it.

The chairperson was not unaware of the comments made about her. Despite their having elected her to the position, the teachers distrusted her. She no longer belonged to their ranks, but hovered somewhere between them and the administration. Consequently, teachers began treating her differently, attempting to manipulate her, or putting her in compromising positions. Although she tried to use her power to care for faculty in order to empower them through the development of SBM, they evidenced anger and resentment with each attempt she made to improve her leadership skills. They perceived her use of power to benefit only herself; they did not link her leadership with their good. Her leadership position contributed to increased isolation and mistrust by both groups. Although they chose her to "lead" in the development of the SBM process, they were ambivalent about what control and authority she was to take and what they wanted to take. Her job, difficult in its own right, became even harder as she expended energy to sift through the criticism in order to pursue empowerment for teachers.

> A lot of [teachers] say about me, "There goes 'The Suit'" [calling attention to her dressing more professionally since she took the position of SC chairperson]. Everybody sees [seeking mentoring from Mattie] as . . . "she just wants to be an administrator, too." They don't realize I'm working for *them* [emphasis hers]. It's hard to empower people who don't want to be empowered. . . . [Teachers] would present issues at lunch time, trying to manipulate me by putting me in a position of having to take a stand for or against an issue the steering committee was discussing and that was maybe going to come up to the whole faculty. There wasn't any more light conversation. Now I'm pretty much left alone at this point. They don't trust me because of my position. They can't connect me with any particular group.

Again, a lack of trust among themselves prevented faculty members from caring and being cared for.

One of the original members of the steering committee ended the year feeling frustrated and alienated from some of the teachers. He felt that as a member of the SC, he had pushed too hard to make changes, changes that would give teachers more decision-making power and more support from administration. He found out, however, that the teachers wanted the policies, but did not want the work and responsibility of carrying them out. They wanted the SC to "take care of it." Teachers wanted particular policies, as long as they were exempt when the regulations affected them personally. He questioned, "What do you do with teachers who do not follow the rules? What happens if you make a rule and nobody follows it?"

His comment indicated particular frustration, for the "you" in the comment, "you make a rule," referred to the whole staff. That is, the steering committee presented an initiative from a teacher or committee of teachers, but the steering committee per se did not decide whether it would be effected; the staff did. Yet, in too many instances, the staff voted for a policy, but did not want the responsibility of enforcing it; they tacitly assumed enforcement was the SC's purview. The following is illustrative of the confusion faced by the SC and the teachers.

The staff voted for a policy stipulating that anyone attending DHS on a regular basis—students, all staff, and university people—must wear an identification badge. The intent was to ensure a safer environment by keeping out persons, particularly dropouts and graduates who were drug dealers or involved in gangs, who had no business at DHS. Teachers were not to allow students without ID badges into their classrooms, but were to send them to the discipline office. Teachers seemed unclear regarding the exact procedures—whether students were to be sent each time they came without a badge, or whether they had a grace period. Teachers questioned who had the responsibility for ensuring that teachers wore their ID badges and that they checked students for wearing theirs. Who had authority to enforce the policy? The teachers generally, as well as members of the steering committee, really did not know who was accountable for the policy—the teachers themselves, the administration, or the steering committee. Or was it to be a collaborative effort? If the latter, how was the collaboration formed?

The teacher felt discouraged and ineffective. He considered leaving his position on the committee, having gone so far as to draft a letter of resignation. Like the chairperson, he desired to use his committee position to enable all teachers to be empowered, but received more criticism and negative reactions than he could, at that time, manage. He felt beaten by the people, his colleagues, to whom he intended to be responsive.

> I think my effectiveness school-wide is almost nil. I have pushed so hard for so many people, now I've got people who are opposing whatever I say just because *I* say it. . . . So I'm just going to back off for a while and say, "Okay, you guys, let's get some people in here to work together for the good of the school. Go out there and work hard."

Another member of the committee discontinued attending SC meetings toward the end of the year, feeling that he was tired of confronting issues on which he could not make a difference. He believed the principal usurped the authority of the steering committee and that no matter what the steering committee recommended or did, it meant nothing without the principal's approval. He did not see administrative support for shared decision-making and collaboration, but only continued top-down authority.

> I don't think I'm interested in being a member of that committee anymore. It's just too much. Too much time, too much frustration. The rewards have been very intangible. . . . I hoped we could make some changes and that we'd begin to share decision-making. And there sure is not any interest as far as I can see on the part of the administrators of sharing decision-making.

Substantiating the committee's frustration regarding the lack of administrative support for collaboration, another member stated with some bitterness:

> I suspect that a lot of administrators look at site-based management like it's psychotherapy for teachers. Basically they're just letting us blow off steam, have a wonderful time going through our little song and dance, and when we're done with it, they're going to do what they want to do anyway. I think they're just playing mind games with us, to tell you the truth.

To add to the frustration, the teachers sought "approval" for change initiatives from the principal before bringing them to the steering committee. They believed that if they did not have the principal's support, there was no point in going to the committee. Members began feeling ineffective, tired, and angry.

> Because of the way things have gone the last [few] years at [Division], it has taken more energy out of me than I am willing to give. . . . I find myself becoming so frustrated with what I see going on and when you ask me what can I do to change it, at this point I don't know what I can do to change it. I can try to keep pushing it [SBM] in the direction I think that that's appropriate, but I really don't see myself making that much of a difference.

That member resigned from the steering committee.

Having to function within an ambiguous situation when others were expecting clarity only increased the sense of frustration, isolation, and distrust experienced by teachers on the steering committee. Caring, for them, required more than an understanding of their feelings. It required understanding the ambiguous nature of their roles and how that ambiguity affected what the committee could accomplish. It required understanding that collaboration and support from the entire staff were necessary.

In Chapter 8, I describe how a team of ninth-grade teachers struggled to delineate their own roles as they worked with one another to develop a project designed to alleviate the dropout problem at DHS. Not insignificant to their project were their efforts to seek support and to collaborate with other faculty members and with outsiders, the community business group and the university. They also tried to discern Mattie's role regarding their project per se and her perception of it within the framework of the school's developing goals. Central to the discussion is the comprehension of caring within a framework of power.

CHAPTER 8

Faculty Innovators and the Ninth-Grade Team

True power has nothing to do with the little games we play with each other. When we know our self-worth and demand the respect we deserve, our power works for us.
— Eric V. Copage, *Black Pearls*, 1993

In this story, the interweaving, or entangling, of power and caring comes into focus. Teachers, administrators, and outsiders—representatives of the business community and the university—wanted to contribute to a caring climate through the development of innovative curricula and school organization. Each group sought power they deemed necessary to enact their caring. The results were divergent understandings of caring and power by the individuals and groups involved. In all cases, teachers needed the support and resources of the other groups in order to effect their innovations, yet they all had their own agendas. Consequently, teachers found themselves in the midst of conflicts for power between the outside groups, among the administrators, and among their own colleagues.

IN A NUTSHELL: WHAT IS COLLABORATION?

Division High was the designated school for many of the school reform initiatives proposed for the Newtown school district. It was the pilot site for a school partnership among business, community, university, and school. Integral to the partnership were the community business committee (CBC) and representatives from the local university (UR). Both groups encouraged teachers to propose various innovative projects to improve student learning. Teachers choosing to work on such ventures needed the cooperation of not only those outsiders, that is, the CBC and UR, but also the administrators and other teachers. Although the intent was collaboration, the partnership projects gave rise to power struggles among the various groups. The resulting tensions caused not only the weakening or demise of educationally sound pedagogy and activities, but also an attitude of futility among some teachers regarding attempts to alter the current system. Furthermore, faculty members felt they inherited not partners, but additional masters to whom they needed to be accountable.

The CBC, having pledged itself to assist Newtown schools in better preparing students for the workplace, offered financial backing and, to a more limited degree, the expertise of the Newtown business community to teachers who proposed innovative curricula. The local UR, formally dedicated to educating all students and to empowering teachers and students, pledged support by offering human resources, expertise in disciplinary knowledge and pedagogy, and, to a limited degree, material resources such as a computer and a fax machine. However, with all offers of support came obligations for accountability, which often were inconsistent among the groups, as the teachers, CBC, and UR each had different goals.

Additionally, the new principal determined that the staff of DHS would develop the mission and direction of the school without the aid of outsiders. Only if the CBC and the UR could support the goals identified by the DHS community, would Mattie welcome their help and resources. The teachers, however, believed they needed the cooperation and resources of the CBC and the UR, as well as support from administrators and peers, in order to implement their projects. Teachers feared that if they did not involve the outsiders in the planning, the latter would withdraw their offers of financial aid and other types of support, offering them to other schools in the district instead. The teachers viewed collaboration as a way to gain needed resources. Although the faculty and principal desired collaboration, they understood it from different and conflicting perspectives.

Teachers' apprehensions about being deprived of the means to achieve their individual goals strained the relationship between the administrators and the faculty even more. Teachers participating in projects advocated by the CBC and UR believed that Mattie, especially, worked against them. They posited that she was threatened by their working with the outside groups. She seemed not to want change. Above all, they surmised that she wanted to maintain total control of Division. A teacher, frustrated because she did not receive Mattie's endorsement to solicit help from the CBC and UR, strongly stated that the principal was "more controlling than she came across," and that she was "resistant to change." Such attitudes among faculty began to grow as a result of previous experiences with the administrative hierarchy, and because Mattie did not explicitly iterate her reasoning for not uncritically and unquestioningly accepting the resources offered.

The distrust that permeated the staff and faculty prevented or greatly limited the collaboration necessary for the projects to succeed. Those teachers who tried to collaborate and who tentatively entertained a belief that cooperation could work at DHS were plunged into a morass of suspicion and paranoia as a result of the relationships that developed with administrators and felt betrayed and used by the CBC and university. They felt victimized in their attempts to do something good for students.

On the other hand, the partnership projects caused teachers to vie for power among themselves. Although several teachers perceived they were victims of power struggles by those within the educational and community bureaucracies, they also perpetrated their own victimization through individual efforts to gain more control and authority. Some teachers viewed the partnership projects as opportunities to advance themselves in the district bureaucracy and therefore sought to gain power for themselves at the expense of the projects and, ultimately, the students.

Some teachers agreed with the rhetoric of the innovations, but refused to take part. Others voted against their peers who conceived new ideas, because they lacked trust in the UR to come through with the necessary funding. Still others feared that the teachers proposing the new curricula would receive benefits—an extra planning period, fewer and better students, and new equipment—they would not. Consequently, they spoke out against the projects, the teachers behind them, and the outsiders who advocated the creation of new curricula.

The story of the ninth-grade team illustrates the complexity of those struggles. One teacher desired to more actively care for students. She proposed a program to increase the rate of DHS graduates by decreasing the dropout rate of ninth graders. Her proposition continually faced barriers erected by administrators, the CBC and UR, and other teachers, all of whom declared caring for students as their intention. Yet, many of the actors, as well as the observers, interpreted caring as a struggle for power—power to control faculty and students. Teachers felt caught in the middle of those with more authority than they, neglecting to recognize those within their own ranks vying for control.

THE NINTH-GRADE TEAM

The Story

This is the story of Marty, a ninth-grade science teacher who believed she cared. Because most students who did not graduate from high school left in their first year, she wanted to find a way to keep ninth graders interested in school. Marty taught only ninth graders. During the previous year, she had written a proposal to the CBC for funding for a science project that would benefit not only the students, but their community. The committee liked the broad range of people affected by her original proposal and encouraged her to expand on her ideas. She then proposed the ninth-grade team concept.

In the proposal, she outlined the need for a teacher representing each of the academic disciplines—math, science, English, and social studies. She outlined the features of her concept of a ninth-grade academic team: (1) smaller classes (25 students) for each of the four teachers; (2) scheduling so the same students would rotate among those teachers; (3) an extra planning period so the four teachers could spend time each day discussing students and jointly planning their classes; and finally (4) an orientation session prior to the beginning of the following school year that would provide time and space for the beginning of bonding among students and teachers. The proposal was met with a variety of responses. The CBC accepted it with enthusiasm. The UR were willing to "jump on the bandwagon," viewing it as an opportunity to partially fulfill their role as a partner in school reform. The principal approached it with an "I'm-running-this-school-and-we'll-see-what-goes-on-here" attitude. Faculty encountered it with a multitude of reservations: distrust of its innovator, of its impact on them, and of the actual, not rhetorical, commitment of the principal, the CBC, and the university to the project. Additionally, each of the three teachers who agreed to work with Marty had her/his own agenda as a team member; none was as convinced as Marty of the importance and viability of the concept per se.

Marty began work with the CBC's approval and encouragement. The UR enthusiastically began helping by assigning graduate students to assist the ninth-grade team members to write a detailed time line and proposal for the development of the project and to conceptualize curriculum implications. With the exception of Marty, however, the other team members were not totally committed to the concept.

At the same time, the principal and the chairperson of the steering committee of SBM cautioned the team that the project had not been approved by the faculty through Fishbowl [the voting body of the entire staff] consensus and that the steering committee had not yet approved it for Fishbowl presentation. Not least of all, Mattie needed to see how every detail of the project would be accomplished before she would support it.

Marty asked the principal if the team should go ahead with the proposal sanctioned by the CBC. Significantly, she was not told to cease working on the proposal. She was, however, cautioned: In order for Mattie to endorse the project for the following school year, everything needed for it had to be in place.

The team held several meetings to plan the project. Each time, members asked Mattie to join them so she could give her input and expectations of them and the project. She never attended. The team members proceeded according to their own plans and hoped they would be acceptable to the principal.

Among the more significant changes needed for the team project were those in scheduling students to rotate among the four teachers and in scheduling a planning period for the team to meet daily. The team members designed alternative schedules for themselves, taking into consideration course requirements other than those in the four academic areas for ninth-grade students. Marty presented the schedules to the deputy principal, who responded that he could alter the master schedule only with Mrs. Johnson's permission. Marty went to Mattie, who indicated that the team's scheduling changes needed to be in place before she would permit the teachers to begin their project in the fall. She noted there was no point in bringing the proposal to the steering committee until scheduling was complete. She advised Marty to work with the deputy principal on the needed changes. Marty returned to the deputy principal with the message from Mattie; he responded that he could do nothing until Mrs. Johnson advised him. Stalemated caring!

The CBC wanted reassurance that the team had support from faculty and administration. The CBC members also wanted to know exactly what their financial commitment was for the project. They began gently, but firmly, requesting that the team give them specifics regarding the time line and necessary resources. Before the team members could respond to the CBC, however, they needed overall approval from the SBM steering committee.

Because the UR viewed working with the ninth-grade team as part of their role at DHS, they helped the team with an all-day planning session to work on the details of the proposal that would justify the project and address Mattie's concerns. They also brought in personnel to assist the deputy principal with the computer scheduling. Significantly, neither of those arrangements was discussed with, or even mentioned to, the principal prior to their implementation. Additionally, the UR scheduled regular substitutes so the four team teachers would have school time to work on the proposal and other academic concerns. The teachers were pleased. With university help, the team proposal would be another step closer to the steering committee and a staff vote. Always concerned with the number of substitute teachers in the building, Mattie, however, did not want students taught by more substitutes and was not pleased that the university had made such unilateral decisions.

Almost a year after the initial discussions of the ninth-grade team project, the teachers met with one of the assistant principals to determine exactly what was required for the project to begin in the fall. As the discussion progressed, it became obvious there was great confusion about the status of the project. The assistant principal was under the impression that it had been approved, that it did not have to go to the steering committee or the Fishbowl, and that the team just needed to complete the detail work. The teachers and the assistant principal spent a considerable amount of time debating those issues. The meeting adjourned with the tentative belief that the ninth-grade team had to present the proposal to the steering committee and, if it was approved, present it to the Fishbowl for a vote. The assistant principal would seek information to verify that.

Two weeks later, the team's proposal was on the steering committee's upcoming agenda. The team members did not know until the day of the meeting that their proposal would be discussed; subsequently, not all the members were able to attend. Marty talked with the deputy principal prior to the meeting. She still needed information regarding scheduling, which she was certain the committee would want to know. The deputy continued to hold firm to the notion that he had no authority to adjust the schedule to meet the team needs.

To further prepare for the meeting, Marty and another team member talked with Mattie earlier in the day, only to learn that the principal would not support the proposal because she felt the team members were "not to-gether." Mattie's comment proved to be an omen. At the meeting, one of the team members spoke against the readiness of the team to begin in the fall, arguing in opposition to Marty's and another team member's position. The team member had not evidenced that particular concern at any point in the preparations. It was the death blow to the proposal.

When Marty could put some distance between herself and the aftermath of the meeting, she reflected on that incident and on the months of work spent on the project. She recognized that although others affected the decision to reject the ninth-grade team concept for the coming year, the primary problem arose from the inability of the team members to collaborate. They did not communicate openly with one another. Each had her or his own reasons for volunteering to work on the concept. They worked as a "team" to further their own purposes, but failed to move as one toward common goals.

Marty intended to show caring for students by developing a curriculum that encouraged students to stay in school, raised expectations for them, and provided teachers with opportunities to help them reach those expectations. Instead, her attempts to care for others resulted in her feeling less cared-for. She experienced the dissolution of her relationship with the team member who spoke against the proposal and who was a long-time friend: "I went to talk to [her] and it just became so painful, I left . . . she even feels she has to leave the building because of this situation." A cold, formal relationship with the principal evolved: "Since the dissolution of the ninth-grade team, she has not even talked to me about it. A 'Good morning. How are you?' That's all I ever get from her."

Ultimately, she felt a sense of futility regarding changes that involved anything but her own classroom. Having worked individually for years on activities and curriculum specific to her discipline, she wanted to collaborate with other teachers to reach more students and have a greater influence on them holistically. After the experience of trying to establish the ninth-grade team, she questioned the possibility of orchestrating teachers, administrators, and outside groups to work together for the good of students.

> I've been here for 10 years working on that Earth Science curriculum, and I've sort of gotten to the point where I just felt like the kinds of changes that I was making in terms of refinement and things that I was doing in my own individual classroom weren't getting that much of a return . . . I felt like I needed a broader support system in terms of change for the kids. . . . That's why the ninth-grade team seemed like such a good idea to me and was so difficult when the whole thing just fell apart. I'm feeling like . . . do I just pull back and do things in my own classroom? So, I don't know. I just don't know.

Unraveling the Story

Through this story we begin to glimpse the complexity involved in attempting to care within an institutional setting. Caring and power are not so easily defined and separated. In fact, we need to acknowledge the possibility of their integration, for authority and control often are needed in order to effect caring, and caring as a relationship involving sensitivity, understanding, and compassion is needed to effect a positive use of power.

In the story of the ninth-grade team, there was the yearning of one teacher particularly to give and to receive caring, of an administrator who believed she was caring, and of two outside groups formally committed to the idea of caring for students. We observed the idea of caring used to gain power, of power used to promote caring, and of caring and power misinterpreted. To better understand those relationships, it is important to understand the dynamics of the situation. In this section, I examine Marty's perception of herself, other teachers, Mattie, the CBC, and the UR in relation to the uses of caring and power in regard to the ninth-grade team.

Marty proposed the ninth-grade team concept with encouragement from the CBC. She viewed the proposed project as an opportunity to work at a school level to raise teachers' expectations for students. During interviews and in informal conversations, she reiterated that caring for students was inextricably connected to the belief that youngsters could achieve more academically. She questioned teachers' and administrators' concern for students because of their seeming unwillingness to modify the current structure to accommodate changes needed for the ninth-grade team to function optimally.

Marty viewed herself as a teacher willing to take risks for the students. She sought the support of the CBC, understanding it as a source of funding, without which there was no hope of implementing a team approach. She included research data in the proposal to demonstrate the effectiveness of teams in the retention of high school students. She recruited teachers to work with her, offering them the leadership role, and offering herself for the detail work. She volunteered to talk with Mattie and the deputy principal to explain and justify the concept. She fought, however unsuccessfully, for changes in the scheduling procedures for the team's teachers and for the students who would become part of the team. She talked with other teachers to gain their support. Finally, she worked with the UR to negotiate human and some financial resources. Each time she saw another roadblock to the project, Marty tried to find a way over or around it. She reasoned that the ninth-grade team had the potential to positively affect students' learning and lives.

By pushing as hard as she did, she made enemies and lost credibility among the administrators and among teachers, including those on the team. Her intentions were seen not as caring for students and, in essence, for the larger community, but as self-serving. One of the members patronizingly said, "God bless her, [Marty's] always been a crusader, always will be. No matter what it is, she has to have a cause. You know? And it just wears you out." Another critically assessed Marty as "just trying to promote herself. She'll never do it 'cause no one supports her. She pushes too hard." Finally, the principal judged Marty as too impetuous: "She has to learn that just because you have a good idea, that doesn't always mean it's time for that idea. She has to learn that."

Marty, on the other hand, interpreted Mattie's role in the ninth-grade team debacle as one of maintaining, or perhaps increasing, administrative authority. Lack of overt support was an indication that Mattie did not trust the teachers' professional judgment. Insistence on a detailed plan for the project was a result of Mattie's desire to be *the* authority in the school. Marty speculated that the principal did not want to take risks for fear of failing and thus damaging her reputation in the district's central office and in the community. Mattie did not want to weaken her power base. In all, Marty questioned whether the principal really cared for students and teachers, or simply used the rhetoric of care to promote her own interests.

Marty's relationships with other teachers and with Mattie were perceived only in the context of one individual interpreting the caring of another individual. None of the actors took into consideration the caring of the individual in the context of her role within the institution: How did Marty desire to care for students and the community in general by attempting to retain more ninth-grade students? How did Mattie care for DHS by envisioning the ninth-grade team as a viable part of the overall goals of the school and of the transformations already begun?

Reflecting on the team members, Marty felt betrayed and hurt that they did not have the professionalism and/or the trust to discuss their skepticism about the project with her. She recognized that she was by far the most committed, but hoped that as they worked together, their enthusiasm for the project would grow. That did not occur. She was dismayed because they did not support change that would provide students stronger opportunities to succeed in school. The team members needed to collaborate in a change process enabling them to work with students on a holistic basis, addressing not only their academic needs, but personal and social ones as well. She was unable to facilitate that.

Her biggest disappointment, however, was her perception that the others had sabotaged the whole project by remaining on the team without a commitment to it. She acknowledged feeling personally and professionally betrayed when she learned that although the other members told her they were supportive, they indicated only their skepticism to others. She experienced the pervasive mistrust that enveloped the faculty, a mistrust so great that it virtually prevented teamwork. When the proposal failed in the steering committee, Marty left believing that more teachers did not really care about students.

> I guess it's . . . so hard for me to understand why change, any idea that somebody proposes, seems to be so threatening to so many other teachers, or why other teachers are not supporting the teachers. . . . If we stood together as a group and supported each other, we could do whatever it is we wanted to do. But we don't. . . . Every time you are suggesting something different, there is a lot of resistance from everywhere. . . . Why is it that nothing, absolutely nothing, happens around here without the most incredibly painful struggle? . . . Nobody ever really cares about what impacts on the kids.

Although Marty perceived the CBC and UR as outsiders, she believed that their help was necessary to the success of the team concept. She questioned their commitment, specifically in relation to the CBC's inability to fund the project in the amount promised, and the UR's lack of support from the administration and a large segment of the faculty. Yet, she relied on them for leverage to advance the project past the principal and the steering committee. By demonstrating their support for the idea of a ninth-grade team through their human, financial, and other material resources, and by their acknowledgment of the concept as innovative and educationally sound, she hoped the project would receive administrative sanction, virtually ensuring its passage among the faculty.

Marty, however, feared that Mattie's passive support—her not stopping the team, but not actively endorsing it—would endanger the CBC's and UR's endorsement of the project. Therefore, she wanted the principal to use her authority to ensure their backing. When Mattie refused to allow her to give the CBC, which would provide the bulk of the funding, the proposal until it passed through all the formal procedures of SBM, Marty interpreted that to mean Mattie did not care.

Although Marty perceived herself as one caring, other teachers viewed her attempts at innovation as a means to gain power for herself—to receive the better students for her classes, to have an extra planning period, and to obtain more materials and help from the CBC and UR. Marty's view of Mattie was that she used her authority to block efforts for change, rather than to empower teachers, enabling them to effect ways of caring for students.

Lastly, Marty received care from, was empowered by, and was a pawn of the CBC and the UR. Both groups encouraged her to think creatively and evidenced belief in her ideas. They empowered her through their gifts of resources to plan for the ninth-grade team. They also used her to facilitate their goals—the CBC to demonstrate their efforts to improve Newtown's schools and to gain some control over DHS's curriculum to facilitate their purposes; and the UR to fulfill what they saw as the university role in school reform.

Marty needed the principal's, the CBC's, and the UR's power in order to effect caring, that is, to develop and establish a program that would increase student retention, achievement, and learning. She needed Mattie's caring and understanding as she attempted to work with a distrustful and fragmented staff. She needed overt, concrete, active support—Mattie's attendance at the ninth-grade team planning meetings; her authorization to alter the master schedule to accommodate the team concept; her explanation to staff of the necessity for, and logic behind, having a team planning period as well as an individual one for the teachers involved with the ninth-grade team; and her call for volunteers to work with the initial team. Or, perhaps Mattie needed to use her power to talk with the team members to clearly state her objections and concerns and her preference for, and reasoning behind, wanting to move more slowly on the project. Perhaps she needed to indicate *her* need for caring by explaining the pressures and insecurities she felt from being in a position of leadership for which there was no model—no one really knew how SBM should function; no one knew how a *partnership* between schools and business and between schools and a university worked; and, most of all, no one really understood what "collaboration" meant.

Although the CBC and the UR ostensibly provided caring for students in a tangible sense, they also wielded power, or attempted to, over Marty and over Division. The CBC and UR could supply her with financial and educational resources that the economically ailing Newtown school district could not. Additionally, they both had political influence in their respective communities.

She hoped that their support would focus positive attention on DHS, resulting in increased funding, a desire on the part of educators to work with DHS teachers to create more effective methods of teaching and learning, and, ultimately, respect and admiration for the DHS community from the citizens of Newtown. Although she became somewhat wary after learning the CBC did not have the money they originally promised, she continued to see the committee as a caring component for the ninth-grade team, for the committee continued to encourage her to develop and carry out her ideas to better serve children.

The university representatives, specifically, brought expertise and human resources that enabled teachers to make educationally sound programmatic changes. More important, Marty recognized their political power over the central office administrators. The university had a national and international reputation for its work in school reform. Therefore, the district administrators eagerly accepted the UR's offers of help to Newtown's floundering, and failing, school district. Because of the political implications associated with that alliance, Marty believed the principal would have a more difficult time resisting the team's efforts if it had the UR's support. Consequently, Marty sought the professional expertise of various university representatives. She also solicited their aid in using whatever political influence they had to advance her cause. Her tactic seemed to be that of fighting power with power, and since as a teacher she had very little, she endeavored to use that of the university. Because the UR were willing to assist her in every way possible, she believed they really cared for teachers and students.

There is, however, another way of examining the CBC's and UR's involvement in the misfortunes of ninth-grade team. Each of those groups used Marty to advance their own agendas. The business community complained that the students graduating from the Newtown schools were ill-prepared to function in the workplace. The CBC used low scores on achievement tests and the continually increasing rate of students dropping out of high school as their basis of criticism. Through a coalition of state government and local corporations and universities, the Newtown business community opted to partner with the school district to strengthen the knowledge base of high school graduates to better prepare them for work in the community. The CBC chose to assist DHS teachers with funding and moral support that would allow the latter to generate innovative programs that particularly provided transition from school to work, thus, benefiting students and the community.

By controlling the funding, however, they also gained a right for input into the programs receiving their support. Projects at the top of their list were academies directly related to business: the Financial Services Academy, the Technology and Engineering Academy, and the Health Science Academy. The ninth-grade team was an outgrowth of a science project and not part of a school-to-community related academy. Conceivably, it could have been the

CBC's attempt at altruism; the ninth-grade team was the CBC's symbol to parents, students, and educators that the business community wanted to help all students. Thus, the CBC offered support to Marty in terms of funding, but funding far less than originally promised her. The ninth-grade team, however, provided the vehicle through which the CBC could be seen as truly interested in aiding *all* Newtown's students.

The UR, too, had its own agenda. The local university was a front-runner in school reform, focusing on the effect of collaboration among corporations and the state and many of its institutions on efforts to improve schooling, especially in urban districts. Newtown provided a challenge befitting the reputation of this university. Consequently, DHS, as the "worst" school in an economically depressed and crime-ridden city, was almost akin to grabbing the brass ring for the UR. If the university representatives could effect changes within DHS that improved student achievement and strengthened relationships among the school, home, and other institutions, the university's College of Education would receive acclaim and prestige, nationally and internationally.

Marty's project had distinct appeal to the supervisors of the university collaborative. It would affect a large number of students, many of whom were below average academically; it was based on cooperation with groups representative of the organizations identified as partners by the university; and it would directly benefit the local community. The university used the ninth-grade team as an experiment in collaboration and partnership. They did so, however, without really investigating how their work coincided with the mission of the school and with the goals the DHS community envisioned. Thus, the university could be interpreted as using political power in the guise of caring to advance itself.

The incident of the ninth-grade team was one small episode in one school. In it there were teachers who were both victims and perpetrators of power struggles. That episode opened up for question the degree to which mistrust and fragmentation affected the teachers' ability to create a climate where caring could be nurtured.

REFLECTIONS: THE STAFF, CARING, AND POWER

An ethic of caring is "an ethic of relation" (Noddings, 1992, p. 21). There is an "emphasis on living together, on creating, maintaining, and enhancing positive relations"; an ethic of caring "does not posit one greatest good to be optimized, nor does it separate means and ends"; finally, "it does not regard caring solely as an individual attribute," but "recognizes the part played by the cared-for" (Noddings, 1992, p. 21). In an ethic of care, caring is not simply a response to a moment of decision-making involving justification of moral choices; an ethic of care requires continuously working together to build and sustain affirmative relationships with others. It requires reciprocity, one who cares and one who is capable of receiving that care.

As I reflected on the staff of Division High, I saw inadequate communication and fragmentation among the teachers, leading to a serious distrust among them. The distrust perpetuated their fragmentation and inability to work together, preventing or severely limiting them from making changes they professed to want and/or need—changes to build trust among themselves in order to collaborate, to develop and implement leadership emanating from their own ranks, and to develop innovative curriculum for students. The changes they desired necessitated trust, and trust required connection. Rather than forming relationships, teachers appeared to have disengaged, to have pulled back into themselves even more.

Teachers recognized the need to build trust among themselves before they could collaborate effectively to make changes. Yet, the history of the school and the history the senior staff carried with them seemed to stand in the way of establishing trust. They talked, individually or in small groups, about the severe distrust among the staff brought about by fragmentation, lack of communication, and extreme individualism, but would not address those issues as a faculty. The tendency was to transfer their own problems as a staff to the traditional adversarial relationship between teachers and administrators. That is, rather than confronting their own problems and seeking ways in which to deal with them, they resorted to blaming the administration, particularly the principal, for the failures to accomplish what teachers wanted to see happening at DHS.

Teachers wanted support for various projects, ideas, or plans. But they were unwilling to support each other as a staff. They complained about the low expectations for students, but when the members of the math department raised standards, other teachers criticized them and attempted to work against them. Teachers bemoaned the high dropout rate, especially of ninth graders, and recognized the "unfriendly" atmosphere into which the middle schoolers were coming. Yet, when a teacher initiated the concept of the ninth-grade team, no one volunteered, few teachers backed the project, and many worked against it.

They wanted leadership, not only from the principal, but from their own ranks. They, however, were not connected as a faculty, preventing them from taking stances as a group and providing leadership that was representative of the staff. The teachers were divided in their conceptions of leadership, some wanting to have virtually all decision-making authority concerning policies within DHS and others wanting only the freedom to do what they wanted within the confines of their classrooms. To some, leadership implied unquestioning support from the principal for whatever teachers deemed beneficial for students; for others, leadership meant shared decision-making between faculty and administrators, with the authority to see that policies were carried out resting with administrators. Teachers could not agree among themselves on what leadership meant to them and whether, or to what degree, they wanted to lead.

They used the word *support* to imply their need for caring—from their colleagues, from the administrators, and from the outsiders. How did they understand support? Too often, it seemed as though teachers felt supported and cared-for only when others agreed with them as individuals or small groups. They did not see support as the opportunity to explore issues, challenge each other, or work together in relation to each other as persons and professionals who were integral parts of a whole, that is, of the school. Efforts toward building relationships were seen as threats to their individualism and to themselves as individuals. The staff did not function as a unified body.

Given the distrust and lack of unity among the staff, pursuing an ethic of care was a goal that was difficult, at best, for the faculty at DHS. Some teachers attempted to extend care, to be the one caring, but other teachers found it hard, if not impossible, to receive care. Some senior teachers evidenced their willingness to work on change, but their efforts were not enough for others: care offered, but not received. Teachers' attempts to improve teaching and learning, thus benefiting both teachers and students, were resisted and rejected: care offered, but not received. Teachers chosen by their peers to lead them through new ways of governance and organization were verbally maligned and their attempts at leadership were undermined: care offered, but not received.

Complicating the situation was the interpretation that often care offered was seen as power, power by other teachers to take control of their colleagues or to gain "perks" for themselves, or by teachers in collusion with administrators to move up the bureaucratic hierarchy. Fragmentation and lack of communication as a faculty contributed to the invidious distrust that pervaded the staff, turning efforts to care into power struggles. Noddings (1984) states that if an ethic of care is to develop, modeling, dialogue, practice, and confirmation must occur. Some teachers attempted to model caring, but there was little or no dialogue and practice, and virtually no confirmation of their efforts to care. As important, virtually no one seemed to know how to receive care. Most often, caring was interpreted as control.

In Chapter 9, I explore the relationships between care and power as they affect both faculty and administration. Is it enough for staff members, including administrators, to simply possess an *attitude* of caring, where there is a sympathetic or empathetic *reaction* to others in response to particular circumstances? Is it possible for staff and administrators to pursue an *ethic* of care, requiring the creation and maintenance of relationships, the ability to give *and* receive care? How is power a part of caring—or is it?

An ethic of care requires care-giving to be situational, suspending adherence to rules or regulations designed to ensure fairness via objectively judging a situation by criteria applied to all like situations. Does contextualizing caring give the one caring power over others, that is, control over others? Can caring *and* power lead to freedom—freedom for change, freedom for the individual as well as the group? Those questions will be explored with the intent not of finding answers, but of finding directions that will encourage us in the pursuit of equity and freedom in our society.

CHAPTER 9

Caring or Power? A Conundrum

I, who saw power linked to oppression in everything, did not want caring to be about power, and thereby about oppression. . . . I wanted the "ethic of caring" to be pristine, to be somehow beyond issues of power that I considered to be essentially hegemonic and masculine.
                                        —George W. Noblit, "Power and Caring," 1993

Like Noblit, when I entered Division High, I too wanted an ethic of caring to be "pristine." I thought caring and power were dichotomous, if not diametrically opposed. Caring connoted relation, connectedness, concern, giving and receiving; it was harmonious community. Because I equated power with authority, control, domination, force, and, ultimately, oppression, I anticipated little or no use of power in a caring community. I expected power to be as "pristine," in a perverse sense, as I wanted caring to be in a moral sense. That was not the reality I discovered. Thus, the conundrum—the intricate riddle— of "caring power" developed.

CARING AND POWER: SHARED ATTRIBUTES

I realized the complexity of the relationships between caring and power through the recognition that both are relational, reciprocal, contextual, and socially constructed.[13] There are, however, differences within those similarities. In this section, I explore the intertwining of caring and power from the perspective of administration and faculty attempts to effect reforms intended to create a caring community within a bureaucratic hierarchy.

Caring and Power: Relational

Gilligan (1982) and Noddings (1984, 1992) conceptualize an ethic of caring as webs or circles of relationships that lead to connection between and among individuals and that also build community. Effecting power is similar to enacting caring, for both are dependent on the interaction of persons. Power functions like a machine, each cog dependent on the others, or like a web of relations in which each person has multiple connections (Burbules, 1986; Foucault, 1980; Gliddens, 1979). When considering educational reform, policy makers will want to examine the current power relationships, for creating a climate of caring in schools will take place within those already established links, and to ignore them is, according to Sarason (1982), "to court failure." A key to that inquiry is the question, How may the relational webs of power and of caring intersect to form relationships of caring power? A continued examination of the story of Division provides insights into connections between administrators and staff members as they endeavored to cultivate a community in which there was the power to care.

The Tangled Web of Division's Hierarchy. The power relationships that existed at Division developed as an inherent result of the bureaucratic hierarchy, a type of domination exhibited through top-down authority (Abbott & Caracheo, 1988). The use of power to dominate, subordinate, or manipulate through enforcement of rules and regulations (Kreisberg, 1992) achieved and maintained social stratification among the various groups in the school. Each layer of the hierarchy, however, was not cleanly delineated. That is, relationships interconnecting the groups formed an entangled organizational structure in which the groups and individuals used their power to protect themselves and to further their own interests. The pursuit of *inter*dependence and connection to create a climate of caring, therefore, had to occur within those already established, overlapping layers, each with varying degrees of authority or control over others. The union structure is a vivid example.

The union was among the more traditionally powerful factions at Division and, ironically, magnified a split not only between the leadership and rank-and-file, but within the rank-and-file. Historically strong union ties in the city and subsequently in the school district contributed to and exacerbated the various school groups' perception of positional power as negative, and led to the formation and continual shifting of alliances. From a union perspective, member relationships with administrators were intrinsically adversarial. Therefore, any change in policy or practice emanating from building or central office administration evoked suspicion and distrust among teachers.

The union itself, however, provoked power struggles *among* teachers. Although the teachers' union was not supported by the overwhelming majority of teachers, it continued to be the spokes-unit for all Newtown district teachers. Nonmembers accused members of siding with administration to control reform efforts, specifically of "forcing" SBM on Division. Members, however, interpreted SBM as a way to enhance teachers' decision-making power. Multiple power alliances between and among teachers and administrators developed, each seeking to use power to establish a climate in which they felt cared-for.

Dissensions also occurred between and among the unions representing various personnel groups within the school district. Depending on the negotiating packages, the unions intersected to support each other, separated to work for unique benefits, or worked against one another for the benefit of one group. Their common link, however, was the knowledge that they were in submissive positions to the higher power of building and district administrators and the Board of Education. Alliances within and among the specific unions shifted, therefore, to form power bases that individuals and groups believed necessary to provide for their personal and professional concerns.

Social stratification by position existed despite the shifting interconnections of power within the union structure. Teachers routinely had the privilege of choosing whether to acknowledge support staff, thus keeping the latter in a subordinate position. Within the administration, each level was accountable to the one above. The deputy principal and the assistant principals made few decisions without Mattie's approval. Mattie was reluctant to sanction nonroutine requests or activities without consulting the district rules and regulations or her "bosses" in the District Office. Such a defined hierarchy of power reinforced the aspect of control, even as Mattie and the staff strived to create a climate where caring for one another and for the whole school body would flourish.

Finally, Division's staff lived the reality of an existent power structure in which separate, unique entities competed with and struggled against one another for scarce resources—materials, funding, time, human resources. The result was tension between fulfilling themselves as individuals and meeting the needs and desires of others and the community as a whole (Kreisberg, 1992). The challenge Division ultimately faced was to develop an ethic of caring by using the power sources already in place, while simultaneously adapting and replacing them to create an environment in which power would sustain caring.

Using the Known Template of Organization. The organization and leadership in place are ingrained in our institutions, including schools. Even when people want to change, it is difficult for them to do so, for they continue to envision and measure all changes by the known structure. The struggle to implement SBM at Division is an example of this. As staff tried to build community, they chose methods that actually perpetuated and increased the bureaucratic organization. The staff and administration intended to remove decision-making from solely the principal's purview by creating the steering committee and the Fishbowl meetings. New layers of bureaucracy emerged, however, while Mattie retained primary decision-making authority.

I suggest possible reasons for those occurrences. Although SBM was a change in organizational structure for Division, the district office continued functioning as it always had. There were few, if any, changes in organizational protocol between the school site and the district to accommodate changes in structure at the school level. District administrators continued to communicate with Mattie about issues related to school and district policy, budgeting, and accountability, and to hold her responsible for the management of the school. Change involving power shifts to support relationships, broad-based decision-making, shared responsibility, and community building has little chance of success in *one* school; it needs the support of a *district* (Schlechty, 1997).

Mattie's role was ambiguous at best. She was charged with "leading" Division into SBM, with all faculty and staff sharing in decision-making that affected the school. The district administrators continued to view her alone as responsible for the successful operation of the school. She knew her role as leader would be different in a site-based managed school, but she did not know *how* it would change, and no one from the District Office availed himself to explore that issue with her. Her models were those of management by top-down authority; her charge was to collaborate with staff to decide school policies; and the bottom line was she would shoulder the responsibility for all decisions affecting Division. Consequently, Mattie vacillated, offering to share decision-making, but essentially determining when that would occur. Her dilemma was how to care while simultaneously using her positional power to create a caring environment.

Teachers, too, had difficulty understanding their changing roles in a structure developed to bring people together rather than force them apart. They continued to view efforts purporting to establish trust, connection, and community through a lens of bureaucratic rules and regulations and from the perspective of hierarchical organization. The latter was most evident when the staff sought the principal's *explicit* support, rather than the school-wide SBM process—*their* power—to determine whether a proposed project or activity, the ninth-grade team concept, for example, would move forward.

The teachers wavered in their thoughts about shared decision making, leadership, and self-governance. Despite choosing a faculty member to work with administrators to develop SBM, few supported her, and several worked to denigrate efforts at collaboration. Teachers passionately testified to the need to build trust, to cooperate, and to develop a caring atmosphere, but they chose means that maintained the current system and climate: They chose to work independently and they chose not to trust.

Some teachers felt district and building administration simply pandered to their calls for empowerment, placating them by allowing them limited leadership and decision-making opportunities. Others trusted their unionist peers no more than they trusted the administrators. Although many teachers strongly evidenced a desire to change the bureaucratic structure, they were unable to imagine one in which power could be used to care for each other and the community as a whole, and where collaboration was the norm. They consequently limited themselves in their efforts to understand and define caring at and for Division and viewed power only as a means of domination.

Each change the staff considered, they viewed through a bureaucratic model; each problem they encountered, they attempted to solve using the tools of bureaucracy—more committees, more authority, more control. The more Mattie and the teachers attempted to flatten the hierarchy, the more restraints, emanating from both administrators and faculty members, emerged. They had difficulty constructing a caring environment for the school community, as they continued to work within their well-established, authority-based structure.

Caring: Individual Effort. Caring was more easily initiated, however, when it consisted of relations between individuals. Consider Mattie's ministering to individual faculty and staff members who experienced personal crises. On a personal level she listened, attempted to "apprehend the others' reality" (Noddings, 1984), and offered care appropriate to the individual. A web of relationships developed as she extended her caring to others who, in return, accepted her caring. Some, in turn, offered care to other colleagues and students, thus enlarging the web.

Faculty, staff, and administrators accepted and encouraged caring relationships when they were obviously not linked to the political, that is, involving changes affecting the established bureaucracy. Mattie's development of grief counseling received little, if any, opposition. Not everyone was required to participate, for staff members volunteered to work with the students or faculty who needed their help. The majority of faculty limited their caring to allowing students to attend grief counseling sessions.

Caring for individuals did not have an impact on group power relations. Caring on a personal level *did not require* the collective staff to act within an ethic of caring. Although Mattie asked some faculty members to extend warmth and concern to those in personal crisis, they could choose to do so or not. In the case of grief counseling, the program functioned sufficiently within the power structure to allow those who did not choose to be care-givers to abide by regulations set up for the program. Since the program required little of staff members, compliance was not difficult, even for those who may not have totally supported the idea. Staff did not experience coercion.

The conundrum of the intersection between caring and power, however, arose with the implementation of grief counseling. One could say Mattie used her power, her authority and control, to institute a program based on an ethic of caring. By embedding it in the power structure, but not disturbing the power relations, Mattie received support for the program. One could debate, however, whether the teachers acted from the perspective of an ethic of caring or from that of bureaucratic principles, that is, in compliance with rules. The means may have been open to varying interpretations, but the end result was caring.

Caring: A Collective Effort. Before continuing, it is necessary to examine the issues related to an ethic of care as a *collective* issue, one involving all persons, males and females, in the community. A primary concern among feminists is that an ethic of caring too often is viewed as a female ethic and, consequently, closely linked with the private sphere. Women are expected to be care-givers in the home, sacrificing themselves for their families. Feminist concerns, therefore, arise from the belief that employers will expect transference of that sacrificial caring from the private domain to the public. That is, as long as women shoulder the efforts required to care in the public sphere, caring will be encouraged and supported.

Caring as a collective effort, however, presumes an integration of males into caring work. In actuality, women continue to be the primary care-givers in the workplace. The bulk of workers using the Family Leave Act are women. Another example is Ghiloni's (1987) study of corporate women hired to manage personnel and public relations departments because of their expert interpersonal skills. Their supervisors and co-workers saw that work as significantly less important than that of others, mostly males, who made aggressive business deals. Extrapolate those incidents to Mattie's decisions. As long as she confined caring to her own efforts, or to efforts involving volunteers, most of whom were women, she received tacit approval from the staff.

Caring as a collective effort is difficult, for it becomes a *politics* of caring, disturbing traditional male–female relationships and, more important, challenging the presumed "femaleness" of caring. To create schools in which caring is the norm, requires purposefully disturbing the web of power relations with the interweaving and intersecting of caring. That requires reconceptualizing power to include a caring dimension. To do that, involves the following:

1. integrating the private—historically understood as women's caring work—and the public—traditionally viewed as men's task accomplishment;
2. valuing caring (affective, feeling) commensurate with doing (task accomplishment);
3. focusing on the *continuum* of human characteristics rather than on a *dichotomy* of attributes labeled either male or female and, thus, categorizing and ultimately polarizing doing and caring.

To understand the concept of power differently requires addressing the dichotomies set up by the notion of caring as female. Such a view distances women (and minorities) from men by polarizing characteristics associated with them: private/public, connection/separation, relation/autonomy, community/ individual, particular/universal, and caring/power. Implied within those is a judgment: Elements associated with males have value, and those associated with females are of lesser or no value. By creating oppositional values, maintenance of power relationships that keep those in power separate from those with less or very little is maintained.

Burbules (1986) stated that power relations change those who occupy them, restricting their autonomy and narrowing their horizons. The few teachers at Division who attempted to work collaboratively with peers faced attitudes of distrust. Having experienced reinforcement of their positions in the hierarchy and the values associated with bureaucracy, and seeing no model for "school as a caring community," many teachers talked about community and cooperation, but strived to gain more independence and autonomy. They viewed SBM as a way of gaining more power not necessarily as a group, but as individuals.

Ironically, they restricted their autonomy by interpreting changes, which had the potential for a greater degree of self-governance and independence, through traditional bureaucratic relations. To each change proposed, teachers responded with distrust and cynicism, and within the limitations they were accustomed to fighting. They worked hard, for example, to develop a program to ensure greater safety in the building by requiring all students and staff to wear ID badges. The faculty, however, were unwilling to assume responsibility for carrying the program out. Several reasons surfaced for their inaction. The faculty did not trust the administrators to allow them to take responsibility for the program. They were unsure of *how* to carry it out and therefore fell back on the bureaucratic tradition of "it's the administrators' duty" to enforce policy.

Finally, the faculty were uncomfortable working within the ambiguity of SBM, and they did not know how to work collaboratively with the administrators to determine how to use the power that SBM provided them. Their action—or inaction—resulted in Mattie's insistence that they determine how to manage the program. The teachers perceived that as coercion to complete their own initiative. They did not, or could not, trust their peers. Unable to cooperate with and collaborate among themselves, they resisted joining together to support those whom they elected to leadership positions.[14]

Faculty limited their vision of change by continuing to view the principal as an adversary. Rather than determining how they could work with Mattie, they retreated into the familiarity of the traditional hierarchy, expecting her, as the administrator, to effect changes, only vaguely identified, that would transform DHS into a premier school. When those "miracles" did not occur within a few months of her arrival, teachers complained that Mattie had failed them.

The faculty presumed care *from* Mattie, but had a difficult time caring *for* her. She needed them to understand the ambiguity of her position and that she—and they—needed time to accomplish goals to improve Division. Had the teachers simply backed the SC chairperson, Mattie may have felt their support in exploring SBM together. Instead, they chose to criticize her for not leading and to detail reasons why they could not. Because of their inability to see beyond the past to a relationship with administrators that was collaborative, and to a power that could effect a climate fostering and sustaining care for all, they narrowed their own horizons.

Mattie also questioned her position in the power structure. How to use her positional and personal power to care for individuals, including herself, and the staff as a whole, presented tensions for her. She wanted to succeed as an administrator and to meet the needs of the school community. Did one necessarily exclude the other?

Initially, Mattie chose to embark on goals most important to her: to converse individually with all faculty and staff, visit their classrooms, be in the halls, and be in the office to greet staff as they arrived in the morning—all because she wanted them to know she cared. Within a few months, staff complained because she was becoming less and less available. She was out of the building at district meetings; her office door was closed most of the day, presumably because she had conferences; teachers had to make appointments to talk with her.

Was she overly ambitious in her initial thoughts about the ways she could handle her job? Perhaps she did not realize the extent of the district administrators' requirements of her in terms of out-of-building obligations. On the other hand, perhaps she was caught in the bureaucratic machine. If she wanted to succeed, that is, receive recognition and promotion in the organization, she needed to meet the objectives of those who had power over her.

Her goal had been to become a principal. She progressed through the "system" and knew how it worked. She desired to build trust and community at Division, but she also chose to abide by the rules, informal as well as formal, of the bureaucracy. She strived to create harmony and trust among teachers and administrators, and to collaborate with them. Those changes, however, had to fit within the established hierarchy. Additionally, they could not threaten her position or challenge her bosses' individual or collective wisdom. The in-school suspension proposal provides an example.

One of Mattie's priorities as a new principal was to decrease the number of students who were suspended from school. Faculty members suggested an in-school suspension program to keep students off the streets, in school, and receiving help with their homework. Mattie, however, did not work with them to implement the program. She would not risk opposing the mandate of no budget increases in order to negotiate with the superintendent to find a way—perhaps some dollars—to at least pilot a program that she and many teachers believed was critical to improving students' educational opportunities. She would not use the potential power she had as the first woman—and the first black woman—to put pressure on the superintendent to show more than verbal support of Division's efforts to create a caring environment.[15] One could say that Mattie was more concerned with maintaining the power relations as an end in itself.

Division's staff struggled with the dichotomies of individualism/autonomy/separation and relation/connection/community. As a collective—a faculty, an administration, and a total staff—people at the school had a difficult time working together; they appeared to fear connection for it might bring loss of autonomy; and they balked at community because they did not trust their peers or those at other levels of the traditional hierarchy. As a collective, giving and receiving care proved troublesome, for that implied a willingness to work together, to trust.

Caring and Power: Reciprocal

Power often is not considered a relational concept, that is, persons perceive an act of power as something being done to or for another person with the one exerting power solely being in control. However, like caring, the perception of power and its consequences result from the interaction of the one using power and the one who is the recipient of that act of power. In this section, I discuss the reciprocal nature of power and of caring.

Reciprocity: Leading to Synergy. The conundrum posed by caring and power increases in complexity with the realization that both require, and are affected by, reciprocity. Noddings (1984) describes the reciprocal relationship of caring as one in which the one caring understands the needs of the cared-for and responds in a way to aid the other to achieve his or her goals. The cared-for, in turn, acknowledges the receipt of the care offered. Each is affected and enhanced by the other.

Power as reciprocal is similar. Unless it is purely domination through which all social relationships are destroyed, power "seek[s] to maintain at least a surface legitimacy to the relation itself" (Burbules, 1986, p. 100). Tension between compliance and resistance is necessary in order to maintain power connections. Seeking to sustain the relationship constrains the alternatives of the person with power, for she must allow for a range of autonomy, including some resistance, to maintain the involvement of the person with less power. Without the tension between compliance and resistance, there would be either consent, involving no conflict and, therefore, no power relation, or domination, through which all social relations are destroyed. Those with power, then, affect and are affected by those with less or without power. Mary Parker Follett (1942) describes the relationship in terms of a tennis match.

> A serves. The way B returns the ball depends partly on the way it was served to him. A's next play will depend on his own original serve plus the return of B, and so on and so on. . . . A genuine interweaving and interpentrating by changing both sides creates new situations. (Follett, quoted in Kreisberg, 1992, p. 79)

In Follett's description of the reciprocity of power, one also can sense a synergy in which the use of power has the potential to free and enable persons, affording them the capacity to implement (Baker Miller, 1976). Power exercised in that manner becomes caring power; it has the potential to become a "blossoming experience" (Follett, 1942, p. 111). The story of the math department, its chairperson, and senior members illustrates an attempt to effect caring power.

The Math Department: Toward Caring Power. The math teachers appeared to have achieved a semblance of caring power within their department. They met regularly to discuss their classes, to help "rookies" new to teaching and to the department, and to discuss, negotiate, and come to consensus about the curriculum and standards. Unlike most of the other departments, the math teachers met not only formally as a group, but informally each morning prior to school in order to chat and to discuss any issues that concerned them individually or as a whole. Mornings were also a time to just "keep in touch" on a personal level. Fridays they met for drinks at a local pub to recap the week and unwind. A math teacher described the department as "our own little family. We're a close-knit and strong department. We have to be in order to survive."

This "little family" did not just happen, but was consciously fostered by the chairperson and by the senior members of the department. There was an unspoken agreement that they would "talk back and forth to know what and how each other is teaching." That seemed necessary to maintain common and agreed-upon standards, and to support each other through the waves of criticism from other departments, staff members, and administrators who thought the standards were too high.

> I can't speak for other [departments], but I can for this one. If we come to a consensus, then we will abide by what we've decided. The whole department will work as a unit. We decided 2 years ago that it was time to hold these kids responsible for accomplishing something before we gave them a passing grade in mathematics. And though we have received a great deal of flack because our failure rate is so high,

we've still held the line and said if they don't do it, they don't deserve
to pass.

They shared the belief that math is sequential; therefore, each of them
adhered to the standards so the students were prepared for the next class. If a
teacher received students who were unprepared, she or he looked up the math
teacher who had them the previous semester and demanded to know why the
students had been passed to the next level. Colleagues did not view that as
misuse of power, but as a "set of checks and balances" to maintain the integrity
of the department. The following conversation between a veteran math teacher
and a less experienced, relative newcomer to Division illustrates that shared
understanding and camaraderie.

> This is the way we keep tabs on ourselves and help each other if there
> are problems. Most of us are comfortable enough to talk about our
> problems, but sometimes the new people aren't. Take [Jim], for in-
> stance. The first semester he was here he let the administration get to
> him. He passed kids he shouldn't have. And when some of us got his
> kids second semester and they couldn't pass the first test, which was re-
> view, we were kinda tough on him. But, we straightened him out.
> (laughing)

> > They [the senior math teachers] were really rough on me my
> > second semester. I had been told by the administration that I shouldn't
> > hold kids to the standards the math department set up. I mean if a kid
> > didn't cause any problems and came to class every day I should pass
> > him. Well [Susan, the chairperson] sat me down and explained to me
> > what the math department expected. I didn't lower my standards ini-
> > tially, but just gave more extra credit so they'd pass, even though they
> > failed the tests. Well these guys [the senior math teachers] got my kids
> > [second semester] and they couldn't do the work. [Susan] and [Joe, se-
> > nior teacher] really got on my case, but they helped me think through
> > how to teach so students would pass the tests. And they also convinced
> > me I wasn't doing a student a favor by letting him pass when he really
> > couldn't do the work—even if the administration wanted me to do
> > that. The people in this department stood behind me when I legiti-
> > mately failed more students that next semester.

Jim perceived the experience as an initiation into the norms and values
of the department. He also indicated that people in the department would
"stick their necks out" for each other. Caring occurred through the support
given and received by each of the math teachers to support consensus within

the department. In Noddings's terms, the department worked out a reciprocal relationship among its members.

Department members recognized a leader's role in creating and sustaining caring. Their chairperson strived to meet those expectations. One teacher commented that the chairperson "tries to match courses and interests so we get at least some of the things we want to teach." Teachers new to the staff were not "stuck" with all the classes those with more seniority did not want. Another member said the chairperson would "really go to bat" for the math faculty, doing all that was possible to support the individual teachers and the department as a whole. The chairperson modeled caring. On several occasions I heard the chairperson sharing information informally with other math teachers; I saw senior teachers working with newer math teachers; and I observed one math teacher asking another for help with particular students or with a new method or concept he was teaching.

Caring occurred by teachers acknowledging the importance of the personal in professional relationships. Through social activities, each person grew to know others as unique personalities. Colleagues worked together as individuals and as part of a community (department). No one person was solely the one caring or the one cared-for, but the roles seemed to shift as needed. Reciprocity was successful because the teachers were willing to be care-givers *and* care-receivers.

Because her position as chairperson in the bureaucratic hierarchy legitimized her authority, department members looked to Susan to care for them as members of a collective. They believed she would do what was best for them as a whole to put their interests as a department above those of the bureaucracy of the school, and even above the math hierarchy within the district. Reciprocity evolved as they collaborated to reach consensus about what they could and would support, and because the staff supported the department head in the interactions and relationships in which she represented them.

Power was not absent from the act of caring. As the young teacher noted, the senior teachers gave him a "rough time" until he complied with the established norms of the department. He indicated that he agreed with the norms, but had a difficult time enacting them because of the "pressure some of the administrators put on me." He explained that by "rough" he meant that the senior teachers kept asking him to justify his reasons for passing students who could not do the work; they also helped him rethink how he taught. "Power" in that instance supported him and brought him into the community of the department.

The chair also exerted power when she planned the schedule. She gave preference to senior faculty in terms of their having upper-level classes. However, by rotating some of the upper-level classes, she ensured that the less experienced teachers had opportunities to teach classes they wanted.

She used her power as a chairperson to mentor new faculty members. She talked to them about their teaching, suggesting methods and ways of thinking that might help them improve. At the same time, she provided an opportunity for discussion in a nonthreatening way. Members of the department respected Susan. Because of that, she could use her positional power to diffuse disagreements among staff and to encourage them to "talk it out." The math department was not perfect, but it did seem to reflect not only an ethic of caring, but the power necessary to work within that ethic.

Reciprocity: A Means of Constraint. Power, on the other hand, has the capacity to restrain and maintain the advantage of one person or group over another. Mattie's relationship with the deputy principal, particularly, exhibited strong control and preservation of her power position. Although she could offer concern for him on a personal level, as during the aftermath of a student's violent death, she was not as sensitive to him professionally. Her relationship with him was such that he was uncomfortable asking her for help. He did not see her as a mentor, but as his superior, one who had power over him.

Among his biggest frustrations was Mattie's unavailability to him. He complained that he had questions he wanted to ask her, but she was so often in meetings and didn't want to be disturbed. By the time she was free, he was on cafeteria duty. When he was free to seek her out, "she's got her coat and hat on and is on her way out of the building. Then I have to wait 'til the next day and it's the same thing all over again."

She offered help in general, but failed to provide specific help, allowing him to struggle and, perhaps, even fail. As he agonized over the master schedule—"I'm clawin' and stretchin'"—a task he had never done, she offered no help, and he would not ask her for any. Asked who gave him help, he mentioned a counselor at another high school. He did say, "But Mrs. Johnson told me she was available." I asked him what that meant. He gave a startled response, sat back in his chair, grinned at me, and was very quiet. Then, "I guess . . . available."

He discussed his frustration as he worked on the schedule with no guidance. He emphasized how stressful the time was. At one point, he puzzled about why Mrs. Johnson did not help him, for he was confident she saw his stress. He said he tried to see the positive, that she believed that if he learned on his own, he would really learn. He reiterated that she told him she was available, but never actually offered her assistance to him. Because he did make many mistakes, he lost credibility and trust among the teachers. Mattie's allowing him to flounder kept him strongly under her control.

Mattie's actions toward the deputy and assistant principals illustrate uses of power as reciprocal relations that were both oppressive and caring. The deputy had a difficult relationship with Mattie. He did not view her as his mentor, preferring to avoid asking her for help. The less time she made for him, the less he tried to confer with her. Their relationship became one of unspoken resistance and compliance. Mattie knew how much pressure she could exert—through silence or explicit requests—and the deputy knew how much he could resist in order to retain power over the degree of compliance he would give. The assistant principals, however, sought her help and received it. They felt nurtured and mentored. Both stated that Mattie was responsible for their being in their current positions and assisted them in developing skills needed to become higher-level administrators. They trusted her, and she entrusted them with more responsibilities.

Caring and Power: Contextual

Context also affects the interrelationship of caring and power and the complexity of that connection. Noddings (1984) refers to an ethic of caring as an ethic of morality, for the focus of the relation is on meeting the other person morally. From a feminist approach, such meeting presumes the "uniqueness of human encounters" (Noddings, 1984, p. 5), thus implying that caring is thinking and acting in response to "particular needs and feelings" (p. 27) arising from specific situations.

The enactment of power from a feminist perspective also is situational. Conceptions of power often are examined from an institutional perspective, that is, how power is operationalized within an organizational structure. To situate it more precisely, however, one needs to see power from the point of view of those subject to it. The context of institutional power requires reflection of the one caring

> upon internal impediments to exercising choice as well as tangible obstacles to [the] realization [of power]—and this means considering practices and conventions that may have disempowering effects. . . . It involves recognizing certain experiences as ongoing expressions of resistance to power—"the power to give voice to one's aspiration to be heard is not so much the removal of an external impediment as the beginning of an internal empowerment." (Deveaux, 1994, p. 235)

One, therefore, needs to consider the influence of context on caring and power from both institutional and personal purviews. To morally meet the other, the care-giver must attempt to understand not only the structure and influence of institutional power on caring, but the routines and protocols that induce the other, personally, to perceive actions as empathic and nurturing rather than as controlling. That consideration leads one to question the degree to which acts intended to be caring are interpreted as such from the contextual position of the one cared-for.

W. Newton-Smith (1973) states that love—I would substitute "caring"—has an "undeniable emotive force" (p. 127), which suggests that different persons may require their caring needs to be satisfied to differing degrees before considering the relationship to be a caring one rather than one of various degrees of control. If that is the case, then, not only the context of the situation per se but the situational position of the care-giver and the one cared-for within the context may render caring relationships quite rare, that is, "the requirements [for caring may be] placed so high as to make relationships that count as relationships of [care] a very rare commodity" (p. 127). How, then, can we begin to view caring within the context of power to effect caring power?

Two stories from Division High illustrate the influence of context on the understanding of caring and power and their interconnectedness. The story of the ninth-grade team is an example of the importance of one's position in a situation to the understanding of actions in terms of caring and power. A second story, that of the effects of desegregation on a significant portion of DHS's faculty, delineates the need to understand the historical context and how it affects individuals as well as the school climate and policy.

The Ninth-Grade Team. Marty believed the ninth-grade team would benefit students and the community by decreasing the dropout rate in the first year, thus increasing the graduation rate. She failed to understand Mattie's lack of overt and enthusiastic support for the program. From Marty's perspective, Mattie did not care about teachers or students, but acted out of a desire to control teachers. Marty, however, believed she cared, for she understood what was immediately important for students.

Mattie, on the other hand, perceived her use of power as *protecting* the school from outside sources that were attempting to influence the future goals of DHS. She wanted the teachers to decide the future of the school without the pressures—and temptations—of money. If the outsiders could support the staff's goals, then their help would be welcomed. Consequently, if the concept of a ninth-grade team was consistent with the directions the staff chose for DHS, Mattie willingly would work with the business committee to support Marty's efforts. She viewed her exercise of power as caring for the school community as a whole.

Marty's context was her situatedness in the ninth-grade team; Mattie's was DHS's goals. Their individual situations provided the basis for the interpretation of each other's actions as caring or controlling. Each was unable to recognize positive connections between caring and power, or that power may be needed to effect caring that would benefit both individuals and the school community. Rather than being the "big" or "small" picture, that is, Marty's concerns as a classroom teacher or Mattie's as a school administrator, the context was the intersection of caring and power generated from both segments. The result could have been the creation of something better than each had imagined: caring power as the blossoming of experience, to paraphrase Mary Parker Follett.

Desegregation and the Faculty. Bearing in mind the importance of a school's historical background is critical to an interpretation of care and power. Teachers employed in the district during desegregation viewed caring and power, in part, from the experiences of that era. That context was fraught with multiple, often unresolved, feelings and tensions concerning racial attitudes and biases that affected not only those who were a part of the desegregation process, but others who did not have those experiences. Staff, by and large, segregated themselves in all-school meetings, yet stated that racial relations were excellent. As more black faculty assumed leadership positions, white staff members clearly noted those changes in racial numbers. They questioned the competence of the new leaders, while denying that their skepticism related to race. A young black woman assumed that the majority of teachers at DHS were white, when the reality was an almost even split between African and European Americans. She felt a dominant presence of white staff, despite the "top-level" administrators' being black. Finally, racial relations were relegated to hushed tones in empty rooms away from doors and intercoms. As much as people did not want to deal with their feelings—did not even want to believe they existed—they affected the perceptions of actions of caring and power that occurred within the school.

Clearly delineating caring from power is difficult at best. Both are affected independently by reciprocal relationships, and they affect each other reciprocally. Both are interpreted contextually as care, power, or caring power. However, there is yet another question: Is there general agreement among educators or within the larger society concerning the understanding of what constitutes caring and power?

Caring and Power: Socially Constructed

Different cultures, different peoples, understand and construe caring and power in ways the hegemonic culture does not. Women of color, particularly, have noted that the discussion and debate about an ethic of caring have centered around the dichotomy of female/male issues and characteristics. Those women call to our attention that an ethic of caring, like feminist theory generally, represents only one view, that of white middle-class women. Eugene (1989) and Lykes (1989) detail differences in the interpretation of caring and power that are necessary to acknowledge in any discussion of an ethic of caring as a basis for schooling

Much of the reform literature in recent years focuses on urban schools with large non-European populations and the necessity for policy makers, administrators, and teachers to better understand the students who attend them. To say that reformers imply the implementation of an ethic of caring would be, I believe, a reasonable assumption. However, there is an implicit understanding that there are basic interpretations of caring and power that are valid for all, an assumption that needs to be challenged.

Mattie faced a lack of understanding from some of the white teachers about the background and culture she represented. White teachers criticized her for the effort she put forth with community members, for her continued references to religion, and for the power she, at times, unabashedly used to further the school's interests.

Mattie could have been called a "Mother" (Eugene, 1989; Hill Collins, 1991; Lykes, 1989) in the black community of Newtown, for she was highly respected and influential. She gained her respect by being demanding of herself, students, and faculty; she expected 100% effort and dedication to education and to living a respectable life. For her, Division's improvement was dependent on community interest and support; and the community, in turn, would improve with the success of Division's students. Mattie believed people in the larger community were interested in Division. She needed to let them know she valued them. There was a connection between school and community, but she had to strengthen it.[16]

Several white teachers criticized her for spending so much time with parents, pastors, and other community members, for that took her away from faculty. Their understanding of caring focused on Division per se and the community within Division. For Mattie, DHS's community extended beyond the walls of the school building to include the neighboring areas.

Mattie's religion was her life. Earlier, I used the word *ministering* to describe, in part, Mattie's relationship to staff and students. She saw her work as shepherding students, faculty, and community members not only in terms of schooling, but also in life. She believed it was her duty as a Christian to care for people because God gave her that ability as a "gift." She was "called" to her current position to lead her community.

Many teachers, especially white teachers, misunderstood her position at Division. One teacher described her as being in the "black-Christian-Bible-toting" group of administrators who stuck together and pushed one another "up." Another implied that Mattie used prayer as an excuse when she did not know what to do, rather than as her inspiration to find a solution. The integral place of her religious beliefs in her life, including her professional life, seemed to cause doubt and cynicism among some of the teachers. The cultural congruence of the overt importance of Christianity in one's life was absent between Mattie and many of the white faculty and staff.

Religion is a powerful influence on women in black culture. Eugene (1989) described the relation of black women to religion as one involving endurance, resistance, and resiliency in the face of attempts of personal and institutional domination. Mattie, in her many conversations with me, referred to the difficult times in her personal and professional life when she relied on her faith to move her forward. She approached the job of principal with that same attitude. Her faith moved her forward in her calling to minister to her people. And she determined to use her power to make the move forward possible.

Caring and power are socially constructed. A culture's history influences the way its people understand and interpret those constructs. In the case of Division, black history—slavery and the resulting strength of black women as household heads (Davis, 1983)—influenced the staff through Mattie and the SBM committee head, who often referred to the power of the black female slaves and the strength of contemporary black women. Recognition of the impact of cultural differences is essential to the understanding of caring, power, and their intersection.

REFLECTIONS

Although I began to observe links between caring and power, the faculty and staff continued to view Mattie's or their peers' actions as either one or the other. Persons most often felt cared-for when their individual needs or desires were met, and felt controlled when unique needs were subsumed within those of the school community as a whole. Considering that an ethic of caring "is often described as responding directly to particular persons and situations" (Jaggar, 1995, p. 193), such reactions might be expected.

However, if we can accept that both caring and power are relational, reciprocal, contextual, and socially constructed, we come closer to realizing a link between them. That realization acts to dispel the notion that they are dichotomous and posits instead the concept of "caring power." It also allows for envisioning a framework in which power is used to bring about a milieu in which persons nurture and support one another in order to create a caring community. In such a society, not only individual potential and goals are cultivated, but the good of the collective is sought and sustained as well. Caring power is understood in the context of community, rather than solely as acts between individuals. Caring for a collective, then, requires reconceptualizing leadership and organizational structure from the perspective of using power to effect a climate that fosters relationships that nurture individuals and that stimulate community growth and harmony.

Many questions about the connection between caring and power remain unanswered. How does a leader use caring power? How does she determine the best interests of the group or the whole collective when, as in the case of Division, consensus is rare among the group members regarding what is perceived as caring? What structural organization would support power directed at caring? How does a leader guide her constituents in the transformation process?

CHAPTER 10

Toward Caring Power

A human ethic, then, is embedded in life as lived. Because that life is complex, not simple; because human motivations are a dense thicket, difficult to cut one's way through; because one often has to choose between two goods, not between a clear-cut case of good versus evil, our ethics must be similarly complex.
— Jean B. Elshtain, *Power Trips and Other Journeys*, 1990

You will say that to fight against somebody may be terrible, but to fight for something is noble and beautiful. . . . The fight for is always connected with the fight against, and the preposition "for" is always forgotten in the course of the fight in favor of the preposition "against."
— Milan Kundera, *Immortality*, 1990

In a world fraught with violence, anguish, hatred, and disregard for life, learning how to care for one another is critical to our survival. Schools, traditionally looked upon as change agents of society, are logical places in which to develop communities that have an ethic of caring as their basis. Teachers and administrators would dialogue with each other to determine their respective needs; they would model and practice caring; and they would confirm each other as valued and worthwhile human beings. Knowing how to care and be cared for, teachers and administrators would have the skill and expertise to care for students who, in turn, would learn to dialogue with them and other students, and would model caring and confirm one another. Educators and students, then, would become the change agents for society, transforming their families and others so that the whole of our society would live with an ethic of caring as the core of our beings. Would that reform could be so straightforward!

As with so many past and current school reforms, the ideal, development, and goals of caring are reasonable and laudatory. The reality, however, involves a much more complex scenario. An ethic of caring will be embedded within a power structure that depends on rules, regulations, hierarchy, justice, and ultimately control. It will not be conceived and carried out in virgin territory, but will be located in schools' individual and group historical contexts that often are filled with pain, distrust, disillusionment, and even fear. It will not

146

be embraced without reservation, skepticism, or cynicism; and it might well be seen as another means of an individual's or group's manipulating the power structure to maintain or gain more control over others.

Caring on a collective level requires acknowledgment of its positioning within the politics of the larger society, that is, within the framework of power relationships. The challenge from educational reformers to school administrators is, in essence, to act morally within a power structure that traditionally has been controlling. The challenge, therefore, becomes one of reconceptualizing power as *caring power*, that is, perceiving the caring dimension of power which is needed to envision and enact an ethic of caring as it applies to the leadership and organization of entire school populations.

AN ETHIC OF CARING: CONSIDERATIONS FOR SCHOOL LEADERSHIP AND ORGANIZATION

The notion that educators strive to create schools in which an ethic of caring thrives, most often elicits approval and positive support. There seems to be the conjecture that we all know and understand what "caring" means and how we would like to see it permeate the relationships within schools. Yet, as seen through Division High's experience, caring is a much more complex concept than at first appearance. In this section, I reconsider an ethic of caring from three perspectives: (1) an ethic of caring as treating others morally; (2) the problematic issues of the importance of relationship, especially attentiveness to others and reciprocity, to living within an ethic of caring; and (3) the particularity of an ethic of caring and its effect on caring for a collective. Throughout, I directly or indirectly refer to caring within a framework of power.

An Ethic of Caring as Moral Behaviors and Actions

Creating schools in which an ethic of caring is pervasive requires much more than a feel-good, or even a tough-love, approach to education. To care is not simply to bolster self-concepts or create a pleasant environment where persons enjoy working and interacting with each other. An *ethic* of caring exacts behavior and actions focused on treating others *morally* (Held, 1993; Hoagland, 1991; Jaggar, 1995; Noddings, 1984; Tronto, 1989, 1993). Challenging educational leaders to ground their schools in caring is a moral appeal. The moral issue, however, is not whether leaders *should* care, but *how* they do.

From an institutional perspective, caring involves leaders' "responding to the particular, concrete, physical, spiritual, intellectual, psychic, and emotional needs" (Tronto, 1989, p. 174) not only of specific individuals, but of entire school communities. The moral significance emerges when something is known about the context of caring, specifically about the relationship between the one caring and the recipients of that care. The actual activity, therefore, does not determine the morality of the caring, but "how that activity reflects upon the assigned social duties of the caretaker and who is doing the assigning" (Tronto, 1989, p. 175).

Using Division High as an example, Mattie's acts of caring as principal were less important in and of themselves than were the interpretations of them in the framework of her positional power and the significance of the expectations of her staff in connection to that power. Judgments regarding her caring and its moral significance had their roots in the social and cultural assumptions associated with her leadership position in the traditional hierarchy and bureaucratic organization. Mattie's position of leadership brought with it presumptions of authority and control over others, even as a care-giver. Tronto (1989, 1993) notes that in a caring relationship, the status between the one caring and the care-receiver is often unequal, resulting in some amount of dependency. Because of the implied power linked to leadership positions, educational administrators rarely are able to balance care-giving and care-receiving with the staff as a whole or individually.

For an ethic of caring to become the basis for school reform, educators and members of the larger society alike must understand caring as moral acts and what that knowledge means in terms of leadership and organization of schools. In today's schools, there is little or no room for moral debate or judgment. Decisions based on "facts" measured against established rules determine specific actions of leadership and are declared as political and public findings. Those requiring moral debate are relegated to "'private discontents' outside the purview of public policy" (Elshtain, 1990, p. 138), thus maintaining control by those in power and enabling them to deny the political nature of caring acts.

Mattie's incorporation of religion into the day-to-day school life at DHS, which violated, to some degree, the separation of church and state, is a prime example of the complexity of caring and power as they relate to moral judgments affecting institutional and individual goals. She interpreted her invitation to the neighborhood pastors' association to meet at DHS, her attendance at area churches in behalf of the school, and prayer and hymn singing at student convocations as caring behaviors directed toward improving students' schooling, their lives, and therefore the future of African Americans. Mattie used her position to effect the conditions she believed necessary to care for students. Her actions could be interpreted as caring power. They also could be interpreted as using her power in the hierarchy to manipulate the staff to do what she thought was in their best interests, despite their assessment. Additionally, the current system, deeply entrenched in bureaucratic hierarchy, made debates

difficult between the leader and the followers. Finally, in the midst of institutional ethics emphasizing rules and principles, were Mattie and the staff aware
that a moral debate could take place? Did Mattie enforce her wishes, intended
for the good of all, because she chose to avoid entanglement with rigid principles
that had no latitude for variance according to situation? Did she impose her
decision because she did not choose to defend her opening the public door
(school, separation of church and state) to the private (religion, caring for
students and community)? Mattie's intended caring behavior was a covert, but
powerful, political statement, reflecting the expectations held of her as care-
giver by her superiors, immediate staff, and the larger community that she
served.

Because caring is political, there is need to ask whether a leader's activity
of caring for a collective (for the good of those within a school) raises moral
questions in and of itself, as the presumption of leading implies dominance
and subordination in current organizational structure. That gives impetus to
question the necessity of attending to others' needs and how the relationship
affects the care-giver's interpretation of those needs. Depending on one's
history, experiences, gender, relationships, and/or culture, caring is interpreted
and experienced differently. Likewise, a person's experiences of domination
and submission create and simultaneously limit his or her understandings of
power (Dunlap & Goldman, 1991; Kreisberg, 1992). Recall the numerous
interpretations of Mattie's acts as nurturing or controlling, premised on the
various persons' prior experience with authorities.

Neither power nor caring is absolute, for they inevitably are restricted by
the capacities of those who are involved. They are not properties solely of the
individuals, but emanate from the relationship (Dunlap & Goldman, 1991).
In schools, understandings of caring and power develop from the connections
between the principal and various groups—teachers, students, staff members,
parents, or community members—and between the principal and the entire
staff. The interactions spawn a far different relationship than each individual
imagines and than that which might develop between two persons.

Returning to Mary Parker Follett's (1942) discussion of the synergy that
results in a dyad as the two persons respond to one another, each is always
influenced in anticipation and by the reaction of the other. The relationship
between a leader, who is a care-giver, and a school of people, who are the
care-receivers, is far more complex. The leader may respond to one act or
behavior, but that, in turn, is the amalgam of the number of persons within
the group. The relationship becomes one among the leader, an amalgam of
persons, and perhaps a few outlying individuals. The properties of caring and/
or power resulting from the acts or behaviors are interpreted within the
complexity of that uneven relationship.

Since particularity rather than uniformity is critical to caring, educators must consider the impact on their decisions to care in a pluralistic society of rules and principles as they relate to the concept of justice, to maintenance of the current hierarchy in schools, and to the expectations of and support from the larger community. A major consideration is the moral significance that the larger society awards specific obligations of caring for others. In other words, what will leaders do, or not do, *because* society perceives a situation as having, or not having, moral consequence (Tronto, 1993)? Finally, questions about moral decisions arise concerning authority and autonomy between a leader and staff in terms of care-giving and care-receiving. How do positions of dominance and submission affect the acts of caring within institutions and the interpretations of them by those intended to give and receive care?

Relationship and Reciprocity: Caring on a Collective Level

The relational and reciprocal nature of caring at an institutional level gives rise to several concerns. First, attentiveness and selflessness, critical to a caring relationship, are antithetical to bureaucratic principles. Attentiveness is putting the other's interests ahead of one's own, to the extent of "getting into the skin" of the other to know her as thoroughly as possible (Noddings, 1984, 1992). A care-giver's attentiveness to others' needs requires dialoguing in order to ultimately ensure that the appropriate needs are met (Jaggar, 1995; Noddings, 1984, 1992). With whom does a principal talk, and how does she decide which needs better meet those of the school as a whole and which are more group- or individual-specific?

Recall the different interpretations of SBM held by union and nonunion faculty, by seasoned staff and beginning teachers, and by various members of the SBM committee. There was no consensus for or against SBM; the support for or against was vastly different, often based only on individual benefits or losses; and many of the nonteaching staff, with far less understanding of the concept and purpose than the educational community members, opted to vote with the majority or not at all. Mattie, then, often needed to make sense of the talk and actions in terms of what would benefit the entire school. Additionally, she had to factor in the expectations, overt or implied, of her superiors. Some decisions angered faculty members, others pleased them. Which ones showed caring and which denoted control?

Attentiveness demands selflessness. Yet, if the care-giver ignores herself, how will she know that the needs she identifies for others are not her own imposed on those for whom caring is intended? Furthermore, from a purely pragmatic perspective, bureaucracy imposes the expectation of putting one's own needs first in order to rise in the hierarchy. Being alert to the needs of staff, students, and community requires significant time and effort commitments from administrators, at the expense of self in the current organizational structure.

School administrators may question, as Mattie did, how much they must disregard their own needs to be sufficiently attentive to others (Tronto, 1993).

Selflessness of the care-giver raises other concerns as well. If the self ceases to exist in its own ethical right, there is no real relation. An administrator who is isolated from and remains untouched by her staff, has little reason to perceive connections between herself and them. Therefore, is it possible for her to ethically make decisions that are caring for them?

Second, in schools, caring between an administrator and staff is unequal, for position in the bureaucratic hierarchy situates administrators as dominant and staff as subordinate. A school administrator is in a position of making final judgments for school personnel as a whole. Her decisions, in part, arise from her positional power. How does a leader understand that power in relation to those for whom she intends to care? If her needs are met through her care-giving, as they were to some degree for Mattie, she may be viewed as encouraging dependency or curtailing autonomy (Grimshaw, 1993). Caring could become an easy way for leaders to slip into paternalism, authoritarianism, and even dogmatism (Hoagland, 1991; Jaggar, 1995). Finally, there is no guarantee that a leader's decisions, despite her attentiveness and willingness to dialogue and listen, are appropriate for the community as a whole. Moral mistakes do occur in the name of "caring for."

Third, reciprocity in a hierarchically organized school setting would most likely be unidirectional because of the dominant–subordinate roles that make up the organization. Although Noddings (1984) implies that caring flows both ways in a dyad, caring at an institutional level would have the penchant to flow from the top down. Because of her position and the power associated with it, staff looked to Mattie for caring and rarely, if ever, considered her need for care from them. Despite her willingness and belief in the calling to care as part of her leadership obligations, Mattie's emotional labor for the staff was virtually unreciprocated. One questions, then, the reciprocal nature of the relationship and whether it was truly caring (Deveaux, 1994).

Noddings, however, explains that in a relationship that is not intimate, one that is further from the care-giver's center, such as administrator–staff or teacher–student, the others' simply acknowledging the one's caring constitutes reciprocity. Hoagland (1991) challenges that reasoning, suggesting that a relationship based on "nonreciprocity-beyond-acknowledgment"—the care-giver's having no expectation of care from the care-receivers besides concession of the caring act—makes questionable the designation of it as caring. Caring as unidirectional undermines the possibility of instilling the value of the care-giver in the care-receiver. The political implications are notable. In all probability, hierarchical status would be maintained; the value of caring would be undermined because there would be no expectation for "subordinates" to reciprocate; and caring would remain "an ethic most appropriate for those in a subordinate social position (Elshtain, 1990, p. 184), such as females and others dealing with oppressive situations. As important is a concern that males would not value caring as a moral act, but rather as an act that had the potential to benefit their rise in the hierarchy and as another way to control. Leadership based on an ethic of caring, therefore, requires consideration of the effects of authorized relationship, that is, reflection on positional power premised on domination and subordination (Hoagland, 1991; Jaggar, 1995).

An ethic of caring within an institutional setting requires discussion of reciprocity from a distance, acknowledging the need for caring to flow not only from leaders, but also to them. Integral to that discourse is the notion that a leader's care emanates from her engrossment with her staff to identify their needs (absence of self), and also from herself in relation to them. Not to have expectations of others when she has standards of caring for herself is to have little or no respect for those ostensibly in the caring relationship. "If the feeling of caring is to be totally nonreflective, then it is no different from a sneeze" (Hoagland, 1991, p. 257). Although done in the name of caring, nonreciprocity-beyond-acknowledgment serves only to preserve the dominant and subordinate status quo.

Leaders striving for reciprocity-from-a-distance must reconsider the notion of "selflessness" from a collective viewpoint. A leader's behaviors and actions result from her own ethical right to exist as self and in relation. Hoagland (1991) notes that a care-giver "must perceive herself not just as both separate and related, but as *ethically* [emphasis mine] both separate and related; otherwise she cannot acknowledge difference" (p. 256). School administrators cannot afford to ignore or isolate themselves from difference. Despite the compelling argument to be selfless, administrators must know their own values and morals in order to understand how they may morally act and react, toward and with, the diversity of persons and cultures in their schools. The "ethical self emerges from pursuing [one's] own integrity and goals as well as relating to others; it comes from . . . perceiving [oneself] as one among many" (Hoagland, 1991, p. 256).

Particularity or Universality: Caring on a Collective Level

Explications of an ethic of caring highlight the importance of particularity or uniqueness to caring. In that framework, caring is set against rules and principles that define an ethic of justice. Caring and justice stand as dichotomous, debates flourishing over which is better (despite feminist dismay with competition!). Noddings (1984) opens her exegesis of caring by stating that "I shall want to preserve the uniqueness of human encounters. Since so much depends on the subjective experience of those involved in ethical encounters, conditions are rarely 'sufficiently similar' for me to declare that you must do what I must do" (p. 5). Furthermore, she asserts, "I shall reject ethics of principle as ambiguous and unstable. Wherever there is a principle, there is implied its exception and, too often, principles function to separate us from each other" (p. 5).

Implying binary opposition between caring and justice emphasizes and maintains the divide between female and male, associating caring with females, the particular, and the private; and justice with males and the broader public and social concerns (Tronto, 1989, 1993). Such dichotomies, however, are false, for both require thinking that involves salient features of the other. Reasoning in terms of justice calls for acknowledging and judging the morally compelling properties of specific situations in order to determine which general principles should influence decisions. Likewise, the focus of an ethic of caring on particular persons and circumstances must be based on general concepts, that is, seeing the particular within the general (Jaggar, 1995). Balancing justice with caring, however, can be problematic. Selecting to focus on the particular within the general results in foregrounding some issues and putting others in the background. An ethic of caring makes some things visible while obscuring others, diverting attention away from general features, such as social institutions and groupings,

> that give them their structure and much of their meaning. For instance, care's emphasis on responding to immediate needs simultaneously takes those needs as givens, failing to question their source or why they are presently unfulfilled. . . . Even when one is aware of the presence of both images, one cannot focus on both at once; when one is visible, the other becomes invisible. . . . In care thinking, social structure occupies a place comparable to the frame of a picture one is viewing; one must be aware of it in some sense but one pays it little direct attention. (Jaggar, 1995 p. 195)

Leaders who intend caring within the framework of schools cannot afford *not* to see both the frame and the picture. In order for caring to be effective, school administrators need not only to "minister" to individual needs, but to (1) nurture their constituencies in ways that encourage individuals to question the structures in society that require that particular caring, and (2) work toward the necessary changes to relieve harsh and often inhumane conditions. At DHS, Mattie cared for individual students and faculty members through the grief counseling program. That was the detail within the frame of hopelessness for life felt by many students. In the years since this study ended, Mattie established parent and health education programs for the high school girls and boys with children. She reasoned that teaching them how to care for their children would help to establish a purpose for their own lives, as well as their children's. She began with the details, the immediate care needs, and simultaneously began limiting the particular needs for grief counseling by providing education for living. That, in turn, infused enthusiasm among teachers, for increasing numbers of students chose to be in school. Like Freire (1993), Mattie viewed students as forced out of school by unacceptable societal conditions, not dropping out.

To view situations and to behave in terms of polar opposites, such as Right/Left, progressive/regressive, male/female, independent/dependent, caring/justice, or situational/universal, is to deny that life continues to move "toward plurality, diversity, independent self-constitution and self-organization" (Havel, 1985/1992, in Elshtain, 1990, p. 145). Thinking dichotomously maintains conformity, uniformity, and strict discipline, all of which educational reformers hope to change through the emphasis on particularity that is part of an ethic of care. Yet, by positioning the situational against the universal, they fail to clearly address the complexity of their reflections and of the content of their actual beliefs and actions, thereby seeking to bind everything, again, in a single order (Elshtain, 1990).

For caring to become a valued part of the public/social world, and for an ethic of caring to influence the school climate, some semblance of balance between rules and principles and moral judgments is necessary. School leadership at all levels necessitates dialogue with administrators and staff to determine just rules and regulations to use as touchstones and guidelines for making moral decisions. Leaders need to model behaviors to ensure that persons act in accordance with those decisions.

A significant problem for Mattie was limited, or lack of, communication between her and the staff, the outside groups, and the administrators from the district office. As she attempted to uphold the rules of the district, she also tried to make moral decisions concerning the whole of DHS. By identifying and striving for goals important to the immediate school community, she directed her behaviors and actions toward creating a climate in which the staff could nurture each other, as well as students. Too often, however, staff misinterpreted her intents, viewing her actions as relating only to regulations aimed to control them. Mattie also attended to some rules *because* she seemed to believe in the fairness of them. For example, she firmly believed in "paying one's dues" in order to rise in the hierarchy and felt that anyone, male or female, who wanted to be an administrator had equal opportunities to do so, despite the preponderance of males in leadership positions in the district. Rather than examining the backgrounds and questioning the lack of leadership experiences of two female teachers at DHS aspiring to principalships, Mattie chose to mentor two males who had the prescribed incremental experiences for upper levels of administration. She indicated to the women that they needed more experience as leaders, but gave them no concrete help.

Often feminists imply that for institutions to become more humane and less oppressive to nonhegemonic groups, an ethic of caring must replace an ethic located in principles and duty. That, however, simply substitutes one single order with another. In a world becoming more aware of its plurality and diversity, there is a need to see beyond dichotomies. Furthermore, it is necessary to acknowledge that the teaching and modeling of caring will occur in schools that mirror the oppressive conditions of the greater society. To achieve moral treatment of others,

> [an ethic of caring] must provide for the possibility of ethical behavior in relation to what is foreign, it must consider analyses of oppression, it must acknowledge a self that is both related and separate, and it must have a vision of, if not a program for change. . . . Further, as long as we exist within a context of oppression, an ethics relevant to us must function under oppression. (Hoagland, 1991, p. 261)

An ethic of caring *and* an ethic of justice *and* power. There is the necessity for all of those concepts to work together: caring power that will enable people to be free.

TOWARD CARING POWER

As a focus of school reform, care is a desirable political ideal. It is suitable, however, only in the context of a just, pluralistic, democratic society in which open and equal discussion about needs and justice occurs (Tronto, 1993). No longer appropriate are discussions of an ethic of caring cast in dichotomous thinking—female/male, private/public, situational/universal—and/or viewed as a replacement for an ethic of obligations and principles in organizational structure. To reform schooling, the task of educational leaders is to comprehend the particular needs of diverse individuals and cultures within tenets that serve as guidelines for equitable and moral treatment for members of the school community.

Caring on a collective level is not separate from power, but is an integral part of it. Power of position, of authority, provides the space in which to establish a milieu where there is room for moral debate, that is, for discussion of particular situational needs vis-a-vis principles of fairness and justness (Elshtain, 1990). To facilitate dialogue and discourse across ethical lines necessitates leaders who are "purposefully developed," and "who have moral and ethical ideas and visions" (Schlechty, 1997) that incorporate caring into institutions currently dominated by justice reasoning and power-as-control or power-as-force. The development of that kind of leadership calls for rethinking the *relationship* between private and public, and the "historical emergence of . . . an institutionalized devaluing of private life" (Reiger, 1993, p. 25).

Bridging the distance between private and public, and, subsequently, female and male, and caring and justice, requires regarding care as a particular, situational behavior or act, and involving known individuals within a larger context of abstract justice. To value moral behavior in schools is to grant its political nature and to acknowledge the power needed to publicly legitimate it. Caring historically has been associated with women and the private sphere. Women have been viewed as nonpolitical in their social roles, associated primarily with values and moral judgments. Consequently, an ethic of caring, like women, has remained separate from the locus of power—the local, state, or national decision-making bodies whose aims are to influence the larger society, including the curricula and goals of schooling.

To merge the public and private spheres, necessary to school reform and democracy, requires power, particularly that emanating from people and places typically associated with domination. It means seeking out and developing leaders from nonhegemonic cultures whose roles and power most often are ascribed as informal and unofficial, and uninstitutionalized, that is, not publicly acknowledged. An understanding and ability to care, merged with official power to teach and model caring, becomes caring power, essential to create the spaces for an ethic of caring to become a valued and nurtured concept within the public realm.

The convergence of public and private signifies that "earthly force and dominion" will be put on trial and evaluated "within reference to certain moral ends" (Elshtain, 1990, p. 144). In other words, bureaucracy, ethics of justice, and power-as-force and power-as-control will be judged in a framework of caring for their contributions toward making moral judgments. To effect such changes necessitates leaders who use their positional and personal powers to guide teachers, staff, students, parents, and community members in their negotiation of regulations that are just and serve as standards by which to make moral judgments, not as templates by which to abstract humanity from all decisions. Thus, to care requires power, reconceptualized within a framework of care, in order to effect discourse and behavior for moral treatment of the particular within the universal.

Caring Power, Leadership, and Organization

People interpret power as *against* or *over* someone or something, as *control*, and as *oppression*, particularly in reference to institutional power (Elshtain, 1990; Kreisberg, 1992; Rich, 1976; Weber, 1968). Power, however, is an entire body of practices and expectations derived from the dominant culture and ideology, and that constitutes a familiar and public sense of reality for a majority of people (Apple, 1979; Gramsci, 1972; Kreisberg, 1992; McLaren, 1988).

> It is the process through which the dominant culture supplies the symbols, repre-
> sentations, morality, and customs that frame, form, and constrain what we do

and say, the principles that underlie our thoughts and actions and the broader structures that shape our experiences in the various institutions in which we live (e.g., family, school, workplace, government, and religious institutions). (Kreisberg, 1992, p. 15)

Although people are never outside the purview of power, it does not follow that they are automatically trapped in their circumstances or condemned to defeat (Foucault, 1972/1980; 1975/1979; 1976/1990). Power can serve to engender care. As an amalgam of concepts, caring power enables one to care enough to create the climate—the spaces—in which individuals and communities can use their innate emotional and/or psychic strength (1) to understand self in relation to, as well as separate from, community; (2) to build a community that is just and democratic in its pluralism; and (3) to experience personal freedom to fully be within community. Combined with caring, power can be used to recognize persons' potentialities in more than the abstract. Leadership facilitating those changes is knowing that one can think differently than one thinks and observe differently than one sees (Foucault, 1984/1990).

Caring Power: For a Community. Caring power provides the strength to nurture a whole community. Leaders use the power of their positions to generate an environment in which trust develops, sustaining individuals and assemblages; to construct and share knowledge within and among groups; to recognize the personal and institutional histories that affect people's ability to care; and to accept the notion of multiple understandings and interpretations of caring. Critical to this type of leadership is the ability to see oneself as part of the community, yet removed. Being both separate from and part of a school allows interpretation and mediation of the staff's, students', and community members' experiences to be at the center of leadership inquiries into the why and how of power and caring. A leader is capable of focusing not only on the external and tangible objects that control her and others, but on the internal impediments to the school community's ability to make choices for their personal and communal benefit. By providing needed resources and supporting innovative ideas, particularly when they do not reflect the hegemonic notions, she uses her personal and positional power to create a climate that allows others to take risks to bring about change.

The diversity of school populations calls for leadership that attends to particular situations without losing site of the larger social context that causes (has caused) them to occur. Administrators question what precipitates particular needs for caring rather than focusing on the individual as the instigator for care. Leaders use their power to discover new ways of understanding themselves and others, and to redefine their practices and desires within a traditionally resistant culture. School leaders capable of caring power see the picture *and* the frame.

Leadership for a collective questions the need to take control so that, ultimately, others may have autonomy. By avoiding hierarchies of expertise and not granting more structured forms of knowledge that can provide resources that some persons have while others do not, leaders keep staff in dependent relationships. Balancing caring with power assumes the centrality of principles of equality and mutuality, but perceives the constant need to interpret and reinterpret them (Grimshaw, 1993).

Finally, leaders who have power to care do not command, but suggest, are listened to, begin something, and see it occur. They "affirm, shape, and guide a collective decision—but [they] cannot enforce [their] will on the group or push it in a direction contrary to community desires" (Starhawk, in Kreisberg, 1992, p. 69). Most important, power of the leaders can be revoked by the community.

Caring Power: Gender-Neutral. A dichotomy between the private and the public continues to exist. Women, primarily, discuss school reform in terms of caring, while a preponderance of men speak in terms of power, albeit in the form of empowerment. Empowerment continues to carry the notion of control, although in the sense of sharing it in a collaborative way or providing opportunities for others to develop or to act. Empowerment, however, does not reach the depth of relationship that caring does. It presumes one has power and becomes the benefactor of another or others by "giving" power to those with less or none. It presumes power is a commodity to be given away, while implying that the agent of power is better or absolved from the dialectics of power if she or he has the ability to bestow power. Caring, on the other hand, not only allows for sharing or collaboration in decision-making, but encourages cognizance of one's position in relation to others and of the effect of any decision on the relationship.

Leadership based on caring power seeks to negotiate choices and goals within the context of how those decisions will affect various relationships between and among individuals and groups within and outside schools. Leaders with caring power acknowledge caring as gender-neutral. They require the thoughtful and collaborative efforts of all persons, recognizing that "we are fragile; we depend upon each other even for our own goodness" (Noddings, 1984, p. 102). Administrators create the space for discourse and debate concerning perceptions of caring and create opportunities for all staff to participate in activities that require consideration of ethics of nurturance and of principles.

Caring power validates the place of women and others of the nondominant culture in the public sphere, giving official voice to their notions and enactments of caring. It also challenges them "to keep alive memories of vulnerability as

[they] struggle to overcome structurally sanctioned inefficacy and to reaffirm rather than repudiate interdependencies as they seek a measure of institutional legitimacy" (Elshtain, 1990, p. 148).

Caring Power: Pluralistic. Writings in recent years about an ethic of caring have been mainly those of white middle-class women. Creating a nurturing environment within schools requires recognition of those writings as representations of dialogue embedded in the perspective of one culture. To expand the understandings of culture takes leaders who willingly open the door to controversy and debate. They use their power to encourage public exploration of conflicting notions of shared social knowledge that leads not to agreement that ends the exchange, but to the exposure of disagreements. Leaders use their power to enable school community members to care for each other within their differing value systems so that the community is sustained and grows because of, not in spite of, different beliefs. Ultimately, leaders who care will open themselves to the feelings, experiences, and even souls of those who have been "powerless."

Leaders within schools use their positional power to learn and grow from the knowledge and experience of persons from other cultures and backgrounds. For example, administrators can learn from African American women how to balance power and caring for the growth and betterment of entire communities. African American women, in private and public realms, view caring as a liberational ethic in which there is no dichotomy between power and caring. Power is a part of caring, enabling the strong to care for those who are weaker or who have no power. "African American women have overtly rejected theories of power based on domination in order to embrace an alternative vision of power based on a humanist vision of self-actualization, self-definition, and self-determination" (Hill Collins, 1991, p. 124). They seek power not for self-aggrandizement, but to better nurture and care for those depending on them. Leaders of the dominant society need to understand their power as an opportunity to re-evaluate and reconceptualize power with those they previously have viewed as the "Other" and, therefore, of lesser importance in societal and political life.

Caring Power: Spirituality. I propose that to enact caring power in a larger sense invokes spirituality. There is the desire far beyond one's personal gain to establish a community that is collaborative rather than competitive, and for which one views self-in-relation to community members as joint guardians of their school/institution/society, which they perceive as an integral part of a global environment and world (Kreisberg, 1992; Quinn, 1992).

Leadership is a "calling," or a "ministry" (Block, 1993; Copage, 1993; Lashley, Neal, Slunt, Berman, & Hultgren, 1994; Vanzant, 1993). One assumes a position of stewardship, not taking care of persons, but being responsible to them as well as holding them responsible to their personal commitments to the community. To be a steward is to be accountable for the outcomes of the school or society without defining its purpose for others, or controlling, demanding compliance, or taking care of them.

To take care of is to treat persons as if they were of lower status and incapable of providing for themselves. Stewardship implies being in service to others, having a responsibility to self, others, and the institution and/or community. It is not to give direction, but to provide the basic structure that will support the self-direction of those who are led. Using power to care enables community members to choose adventure and pursue their own purposes, rather than allowing others to provide the means for their safety and development of self-esteem through visions not created by themselves (Block, 1993).

Schools with Caring Power

An ethic of caring requires organizational structure and leadership that support thinking and doing. It demands time, which, in turn, demands resources, skills, and knowledge. Will a school organization—students, teachers, administrators, boards of education, and, ultimately, the citizenry—be willing to give enough time to change decades of education based on competition, autonomy, control, and independence, in order to cultivate interdependence, connection, and community *along with* those traditional goals?

The staff of DHS was emotionally exhausted as a result of past personal and professional histories, including participation in multiple reform efforts. Faculty wanted immediate results, but realistically knew that could not happen. They feared involvement in yet another reform, for they believed that they would not be given time and resources with which to carry it out. Those experiences and attitudes, however, are precisely the evidence that should persuade reformers of the necessity to allow time, because trust, connection, and community do not develop within prescribed time periods. Caring is personal, emotional, affective; it cannot be mandated, but must be nurtured. As Mattie recognized, change takes time.

Creation and implementation of an ethic of caring in schools requires leaders who do not have all the answers, who willingly struggle with ambiguity, who willingly make hard decisions—use their power—knowing that at some point they may make a decision, unintentionally, that is not in the best interests of an individual or group. They know how to regroup. They dialogue, having a good sense of when to show their weaknesses and when that would be damaging to themselves or to the group. They have a vision clear enough to guide others, while simultaneously working with others to create a collective vision. They are political subjects, understanding the delicate balance of care, justice, and power. These leaders

> appear to reject the authoritarianism of master narratives; refuse traditions which allow only for reverence of what is; deny those instrumental and universalized forms of rationality which eliminate the historical and the contingent; refuse to subordinate the discourse of ethics to the politics of verification; and recognize a substantive citizenship which requires a multiple subject who can speak and act as a critical and responsible citizen in a variety of settings. Such a subject links freedom not merely to individual rights but to a comprehensive theory of human welfare. (Giroux, 1996, p. 9)

Organizational structure is such that it can support leaders in the process of continuous change, from the first tentative, never-before-taken steps away from the comfortable structure of bureaucratic hierarchy, to the never-ending path of personal and collective discovery.

CONCLUSION

The experience of attaining an integration of caring and power may be disorienting. Past guides for behaviors and practices are open to questioning; old patterns and interpretations become subject to extreme doubt. New ways of thought and behavior are not always clearly delineated and may be difficult to interpret. Additionally, to question ostensibly emancipatory theories is appropriate, for tradition discloses past blindness to their dominating and oppressive tendencies (Grimshaw, 1993).

Functioning within an ethic of caring involves the use of power. Caring power is the link to freedom *to*—not *from*; the freedom to become. Caring allows persons to use their inner force to become *in relation* to others (Arendt, 1958; Baker Miller, 1976; Beck, 1994; Block, 1993; Greene, 1988, 1995; Lipsitz, 1995; Noddings, 1984, 1992, 1995). There will be mistakes; some people may be hurt. But change—and freedom—does not come without a price.

A better system doesn't automatically mean a better life—"only by creating a better life can a better system be developed" (Havel, 1985/1992, p. 162).

Notes

1. The name of the school, town, and all school personnel in this and the following chapters are pseudonyms.

2. See Samuel G. Freedman's book, *Small Victories* (1990), which tells of a teacher who cared too much.

3. This is a case study of 11 women who had been diagnosed as schizophrenic. The book documents their cases primarily through transcripts of interviews with the women themselves and with members of their families, especially their parents. Grimshaw discusses this book in some detail, noting that "what really happened, Laing showed, was that absolutely any attempts to achieve any form of independence from parental control or wishes were interpreted as 'bad'; all attempts at autonomy were blocked. The progression from 'badness' to 'madness' was a result of the failure to achieve any sort of autonomy. . . . But the really crucial thing which lay behind this failure was not just the fact of parental control, but the ways (*largely unconscious* [emphasis added]) by which this was achieved" (p. 177).

4. Peggy McIntosh (1990) examines the conception of race and gender in the industrialized West using a theoretical model that she describes as a faulted triangle. The faulted triangle diagrammatically illustrates the "overvalued, overdeveloped, 'vertical,' competitive functions at odds with undervalued, underrecognized, 'lateral' collaborative functions" (p. 6). She associates the former characteristics with the white male patriarchy, and the latter with women and minority races.

5. Of the 35 I interviewed, only one mentioned Mattie's vision difficulty; no one else even alluded to it. Mattie herself described the impairment as looking through a "very scratched window" with one eye; the other eye is weak from overuse. Additionally, she must wear dark glasses in bright light and must limit her reading time.

6. The Concerned Pastors' Council was a group of pastors committed to improving the safety, welfare, education, and so on, of the community.

7. Steering committee members' perceptions of SBM will be discussed in Chapter 6.

8. This will be discussed in detail in Chapter 6.

9. Division High embarked on a program to develop, over a period of several years, "academies," which were focus areas for students in business, science, and other areas.

10. I will discuss this in depth in a later chapter.

11. Previously, I used numerous quotations from interviews to substantiate the issues under discussion. The reader will note that in this section there are very few direct quotations. All staff members who spoke specifically about desegregation asked me to turn off the tape recorder. They gave me permission to use the essence of their

comments, but did not want to be quoted directly. The quotations in this section are from teachers who spoke indirectly about the racial tension that existed at the time of the study.

12. Elementary schools were under federal mandate to desegregate. Secondary schools were judged, at that time, to be sufficiently integrated racially. Newtown, however, elected to develop magnet classes for each high school that would serve as vehicles to further desegregate the schools. Desegregation at the secondary level, therefore, would be locally initiated and controlled, rather than a hasty response to federal mandates.

13. For a detailed discussion of power as relational, reciprocal, socially constructed, and contextual, see Burbules (1986).

14. Foucault (1975/1979) discusses the exercise of power as control through Bentham's imaginary architectural figure, the Panopticon. The function of the building was to "induce in the inmate a state of conscious and permanent visibility that assures the automatic functioning of the power" (p. 201); that is, to put those inside under the illusion of continual surveillance so that, ultimately, those who are under surveillance will monitor themselves. "This architectural apparatus should be a machine for creating and sustaining a power relation independent of the person who exercises it; in short, that the inmates should be caught up in a power situation of which they are themselves the bearers" (p. 201).

As I listened to and observed the staff at Division, I was impressed with the degree to which they maintained the bureaucratic hierarchy and the control it had over them. Dissatisfied with their situations and presented with opportunities for change, they were unable to free themselves to think differently, which, in large part, included trusting one another, trusting that their peers were not part of the "surveillance." Foucault stated that Bentham "laid down the principle that power should be visible and unverifiable. Visible: the inmate will constantly have before his eyes the tall outline of the central tower from which he is spied upon. Unverifiable: the inmate must never know whether he is being looked at any one moment; but he must be sure that he may always be so" (p. 201). Mattie was the visible power. But the teachers did not trust the working relationship between Mattie and the SC chairperson. Perhaps they feared that she was part of the invisible power that "spied" on them.

15. Ironically, a faculty member stated that Mattie was given "free rein" by the superintendent to spend money, money that was not accessible to other administrators in the district, to refurbish Division. That would be in line with the notion of caring as a female ethic—Mattie was capable of beautifying the school, but not of "doing," that is, implementing a critical program for students.

16. In the fall of her initial year as principal, Mattie invited me to a dinner given in her honor by friends and family to celebrate her appointment as the first female high school principal in Newtown. Former students and friends spoke briefly about her. Without exception, they all talked about the high expectations she held for them and for herself; her strong belief in God and how that governed her life; and her caring for them. One person specifically talked about the community's looking to Mattie for leadership to help her people work toward success.

References

Abbott, M. G., & Caracheo, F. (1988). Power, authority, and bureaucracy. In N. J. Boyan (Ed.), *Handbook of research on educational administration* (pp. 239–257). New York: Longman.

Acker, J. (1991). Hierarchies, jobs, and bodies: A theory of gendered organizations. *Gender and Society, 4*(2), 139–158.

Anyon, J. (1981). Social class and school knowledge. *Curriculum Inquiry, 11,* 3–42.

Anyon, J. (1983). Intersections of gender and class: Accommodations and resistance by working-class and affluent females to contradictory sex-role ideologies. In S. Walker & L. Barton (Eds.), *Gender, class, and education.* London: Falmer Press.

Apple, M. (1979). *Ideology and curriculum.* Boston: Routledge & Kegan Paul.

Apple, M. W. (1996). *Cultural politics and education.* New York: Teachers College Press.

Arendt, H. (1958). *The human condition.* Chicago: University of Chicago Press.

Baker Miller, J. (1976). *Toward a new psychology of women.* Boston: Beacon Press.

Beck, L. (1992). Meeting the challenge of the future: The place of a caring ethic in educational administration. *American Journal of Education. 100*(4), 454–496.

Beck, L. G. (1994). *Reclaiming educational administration as a caring profession.* New York: Teachers College Press.

Beck, L. G., & Murphy, J. (1994). *Ethics in educational leadership programs: An expanding role.* Thousand Oaks, CA: Corwin Press.

Bellah, R., Madsen, R., Sullivan, W. M., Swidler, A., & Tipton, S. M. (1985). *Habits of the heart: Individualism and commitment in American life.* New York: Harper & Row.

Blackmore, J. (1991a). Changing from within: Feminist educators and administrative leadership. *Peabody Journal of Education, 68,* 19–40.

Blackmore, J. (1991b, April). *Policy dialogue: Feminist administrators working for educational change.* Paper presented at the annual meeting of the American Educational Research Association, San Francisco.

Blackmore, J. (1993). "In the shadow of men": The historical construction of education administration as "masculinist" enterprise. In J. Blackmore & J. Kenway (Eds.), *Gender matters in educational administration and policy: A feminist introduction* (pp. 27–48). Bristol, PA: Falmer Press.

Block, P. (1993). *Stewardship: Choosing service over self-interest.* San Francisco: Berrett-Koehler.

Bogden, R., & Biklen, S. K. (1982). *Qualitative research for education: An introduction to theory and methods.* Boston: Allyn & Bacon.

Boyer, E. R. (1995). *The basic school: A community for learning.* Princeton, NJ: Carnegie Foundation for the Advancement of Teaching.

Brown, C. (1982). Home production for use in a market economy. In B. Thorne, with M. Yalom (Eds.), *Rethinking the family: Some feminist questions* (pp. 151–167). New York: Longman.

Bryk, A. S. , Lee, V. E., & Smith, J. B. (1990). High school organization and its effects on teachers and students: An interpretive summary of the research. In W. H. Clune & J. F. Witte (Eds.), *Choice and control in American education Vol.1: The theory of choice and control in education* (pp. 135–226). New York: Falmer Press.

Buber, M. (1958). *I and thou*. (R. Smith, Trans.) New York: Scribner.

Burbules, N. C. (1986). A theory of power in education. *Educational Theory, 36*(2), 95–114.

Calas, M. B., & Smircich, L. (1988). Using the F word: Feminist theories and social consequences of organizational research. Paper presented at the Academy of Management meeting, Anaheim, CA.

Chodorow, N. (1978). *The reproduction of mothering*. Berkeley: University of California Press.

Copage, E. V. (1993). *Black pearls: Daily meditations, affirmations, and inspirations for African-Americans*. New York: Quill-William Morrow.

Cusick, P. (1983). *The egalitarian ideal and the American high school*. New York: Longman.

Cusick, P. (1992). *The educational system: Its nature and logic*. New York: McGraw-Hill.

Daly, M. (1973). *Beyond god the father: Toward a philosophy of women's liberation*. Boston: Beacon Press.

Davis, A. Y. (1983). *Women, race, and class*. New York: Vintage Books.

Deveaux, M. (1994). Feminism and empowerment: A critical reading of Foucault. *Feminist Studies, 20*(2), 223–247.

Dillard, C. B. (1994). The power of call, the necessity of response: African world feminist voices as catalysts for educational change and social empowerment. *Initiatives, 56*(3), 9–22.

Dunlap, D. M., & Goldman, P. (1991). Rethinking power in schools. *Educational Administration Quarterly, 27*(1), 5–29.

Edelman, M. W. (1987). *Families in peril: An agenda for social change*. Cambridge, MA: Harvard University Press.

Elshtain, J. B. (1981). *Public man, private woman: Women in social and political thought*. Princeton, NJ: Princeton University Press.

Elshtain, J. B. (1990). *Power trips and other journeys: Essays in feminism as civic discourse*. Madison: University of Wisconsin Press.

Enomoto, E. K. (1995, April). *Negotiating the ethic of care and justice*. Paper presented at the annual meeting of the American Educational Research Association, San Francisco.

Enomoto, E. K. (1996, April). Deconstructing the principalship. Paper presented for the symposium, Troubled Educational Administration, of Division A at the annual meeting of the American Educational Research Association, New York.

Eugene, T. M. (1989). Sometimes I feel like a motherless child: The call and response for a liberational ethic of care by black feminists. In M. Brabeck (Ed.), *Who cares?: Theory, research, and educational implications of the ethic of care* (pp. 45–62). New York: Praeger.

Family leave draws mixed reviews. (1993, July 15). *Journal and Courier*, Lafayette, Indiana, p. A3.

Ferguson, K. E. (1984). *The feminist case against bureaucracy*. Philadelphia: Temple University Press.

Finch, J., & Groves, D. (Eds.). (1983). *A labour of love: Women, work and caring*. London: Routledge & Kegan Paul.

Fine, M. (1986). Why urban adolescents drop into and out of public high school. *Teachers College Record, 87*(3), 392–409.

Fine, M. (1987). Silencing in public schools. *Language Arts, 64*(2), 157–174.

Fischer, F., & Sirianni, C. (1984). Organization theory and bureaucracy: A critical introduction. In F. Fischer & C. Sirianni (Eds.), *Critical studies in organization and bureaucracy* (pp. 3–20). Philadelphia: Temple University Press.

Fisher, B., & Tronto, J. (1990). Toward a feminist theory of caring. In E. Abel & M. Nelson (Eds.), *Circle of care: Work and identity in women's lives* (pp. 35–62). Albany: State University of New York Press.

Follett, M. P. (1942). *Dynamic administration*. New York: Longmans, Green.

Foucault, M. (1979). *Discipline and punish: The birth of the prison* (A. Sheridan, Trans.). New York: Vintage Books. (Original work published 1975)

Foucault, M. (1980). Truth and power. In C. Gordon (Ed.), *Power/Knowledge: Selected interviews and other writings, 1972–1977. Michel Foucault* (C. Gordon, L. Marshall, J. Mepham, & K. Soper, Trans.) (pp.108–133). New York: Pantheon Books. (Original work published 1972)

Foucault, M. (1990). *The history of sexuality: Vol.1. An introduction* (R. Hurley, Trans.). New York: Vintage Books. (Original work published 1976)

Foucault, M. (1990). *The history of sexuality: Vol.2. The use of pleasure* (R. Hurley, Trans.). New York: Vintage Books. (Original work published 1984)

Fox-Genovese, E. (1991). *Feminism without illusions: A critique of individualism*. Chapel Hill: University of North Carolina Press.

Freedman, S. G. (1990). *Small victories: The real world of a teacher, her students, and their high school*. New York: Harper & Row.

Freire, P. (1993). *Pedagogy of the city* (D. Macedo, Trans.). New York: Continuum.

Frye, M. (1983). *The politics of reality*. Trumansburg, NY: Crossing Press.

Ghiloni, B. W. (1987). The velvet ghetto: Women, power, and the corporation. In B. W. Domhoff & T. R. Dye (Eds.), *Power elites and organizations* (pp. 21–36). Newbury Park, CA: Sage.

Gilligan, C. (1982). *In a different voice*. Cambridge, MA: Harvard University Press.

Gilligan, C. (1983). Do the social sciences have an adequate theory of moral development? In N. Haan, R. Bellah, P. Robinson, & W. Sullivan (Eds.), *Social science as moral inquiry* (pp. 33–51). New York: Columbia University Press.

Gilligan, C., Lyons, N. P., & Hanmer, T. J. (Eds.) (1990). *Making connections: The relational worlds of adolescent girls and Emma Willard School*. Cambridge, MA: Harvard University Press.

Giroux, H. A. (1996). *Fugitive cultures: Race, violence and youth*. New York: Routledge.

Gliddens, A. (1979). *Central problems in social theory: Action, structure and contradiction in social analysis*. Berkeley: University of California Press.

Goodlad, J. I. (1988). *School-university partnerships in action: Concepts, cases, and concerns.* New York: Teachers College Press.

Goodlad, J. I. (1990). *Moral dimensions of teaching.* San Francisco: Jossey-Bass.

Graham, H. (1983). Caring: A labour of love. In J. Finch & D. Groves (Eds.), *A labour of love: Women, work and caring* (pp. 13–30). London: Routledge & Kegan Paul.

Gramsci, A. (1972). *Selections from the prison notebooks* (Q. Hoare & G. Smith, Eds. & Trans.). New York: Irvington Press.

Greene, M. (1988). *The dialectic of freedom.* New York: Teachers College Press.

Greene, M. (1995). *Releasing the imagination: Essays on education, the arts, and social change.* San Francisco: Jossey-Bass.

Grimshaw, J. (1986). *Philosophy and feminist thinking.* Minneapolis: University of Minnesota Press.

Grimshaw, J. (1993). Practices of freedom. In C. Ramazanoglu (Ed.), *Up against Foucault: Explorations of some tensions between Foucault and feminism* (pp. 50–72). New York: Routledge.

Hammersley, M., & Atkinson, P. (1983). *Ethnography: Principles in practice.* London: Routledge.

Harding, S. (1986). *The science question in feminism.* Ithaca, NY: Cornell University Press.

Harding, S. (Ed.). (1987). *Feminism and methodology.* Bloomington: Indiana University Press.

Harding, S. (1991). *Whose science? Whose knowledge?: Thinking from women's lives.* Ithaca, NY: Cornell University Press.

Hartsock, N. C. M. (1984). *Money, sex, and power.* Boston: Northeastern University Press.

Havel, V. (1992). The power of the powerless. In P. Wilson (Ed.), *Open letters: Selected writings 1965–1990 by Vaclav Havel* (P. Wilson, Trans.) (pp. 125–214). New York: Vintage Books. (Original work published 1985)

Hearn, J., Sheppard, D. L., Tancred-Sheriff, P., & Burrell, G. (Eds.). (1989). *The sexuality of organization.* Newbury Park, CA: Sage.

Held, V. (1993). *Feminist morality: Transforming culture, society, and politics.* Chicago: University of Chicago Press.

Hill Collins, P. (1991). *Black feminist thought: Knowledge, consciousness, and the politics of empowerment.* New York: Routledge.

Hoagland, S. L. (1991). Some thoughts about caring. In C. Card (Ed.), *Feminist ethics* (pp. 246–263). Lawrence: University Press of Kansas.

Hodgkinson, H. (1986). *The schools we need for the kids we've got.* Paper presented at the 1987 annual meeting of the American Association of Colleges for Teacher Education, Washington, DC.

The Holmes Group (1986). *Tomorrow's teachers.* East Lansing, MI: Author.

The Holmes Group (1988). *Tomorrow's schools.* East Lansing, MI: Author.

Jackson, P. (1986). *The practice of teaching.* New York: Teachers College Press.

Jaggar, A. (1983). *Feminist politics and human nature.* Totowa, NJ: Rowman and Allanheld.

Jaggar, A. M. (1995). Caring as a feminist practice of moral reason. In V. Held (Ed.),

Justice and care: Essential readings in feminist ethics (pp. 179–202). Boulder, CO: Westview Press.

Kanter, R. M. (1977). *Men and women of the corporation.* New York: Basic Books.

Kotlowitz, A. (1991). *There are no children here: The story of two boys growing up in the other America.* New York: Anchor.

Kreisberg, S. (1992). *Transforming power: Domination, empowerment, and education.* Albany: State University of New York Press.

Krieger, S. (1991). *Social science and the self: Personal essays on an art form.* New Brunswick, NJ: Rutgers University Press.

Kundera, M. (1978). *The book of laughter and forgetting* (M. N. Heim, Trans.). New York: Penguin Books.

Kundera, M. (1990). *Immortality* (P. Kussi, Trans.). New York: Grove & Weidenfeld.

Lashley, M. E., Neal, M. T., Slunt, E. T., Berman, L. M., & Hultgren, F. H. (1994). *Being called to care.* Albany: State University of New York Press.

Lipsitz, J. (1995). Prologue: Why we should care about caring. *Phi Delta Kappan, 76*(9), 665–666.

Lortie, D. C. (1975). *Schoolteacher: A sociological study.* Chicago: University of Chicago Press.

Luke, C., & Gore, C. (Eds.) (1992). *Feminisms and critical pedagogy.* New York: Routledge.

Lykes, M. B. (1989). The caring self: Social experiences of power and powerlessness. In M. Brabeck (Ed.), *Who cares?: Theory, research, and implications of the ethic of care* (pp. 164–180). New York: Praeger.

Lyons, N. P. (1990). Visions and competencies: An educational agenda for exploring the ethical and intellectual dimensions of decision-making and conflict negotiation. In J. Antler & S. K. Biklen (Eds.), *Changing education: Women as radicals and conservators* (pp. 277–294). Albany: State University of New York.

Machiavelli, N. (1996/1469–1527). *The prince.* (P. Sonnino, Trans.). Atlantic Highlands, NJ: Humanities Press.

Macmurray, J. (1950). *Conditions of freedom.* London: Faber & Faber.

Marshall, C. (1992). School administrators' values: A focus on atypicals. *Educational Administration Quarterly, 28*(3), 368–386.

Marshall, C., & Rusch, E. (1996, April). Real Talk about Gender Issues. Paper presented for the Symposium, Troubled Educational Administration, of Division A at the annual meeting of the American Educational Research Association, New York.

McDonald, M. (1991, September 15). First woman high school principal brings background of striving. *The Flint Journal,* pp. A1, A11.

McIntosh, P. (1983, October). Interactive phases of curricular revision: A feminist perspective. Working Paper No. 124. Wellesley College Center for Research on Women. Wellesley, MA.

McLaren, P. (1988, Fall). On ideology and education: Critical pedagogy and the politics of education. *Social Text,* pp. 153–185.

Newton-Smith, W. (1973). A conceptual investigation of love. In A. Montifiore (Ed.), *Philosophy and personal relations* (pp. 113–136). Montreal: Queens University Press.

Noblit, G. W. (1993, Spring). Power and caring. *American Educational Journal, 30*(1), 23–38.

Noddings, N. (1984). *Caring: A feminine approach to ethics and moral education.* Berkeley: University of California Press.

Noddings, N. (1988). An ethic of caring and its implications for instructional arrangements. *American Journal of Education, 96*(2), 215–230.

Noddings, N. (1989). *Women and evil.* Berkeley: University of California Press.

Noddings, N. (1991). Caring and continuity in education. *Scandinavian Journal of Educational Research, 35*(1), 3–12.

Noddings, N. (1992). *The challenge to care in schools: An alternative approach to education.* New York: Teachers College Press.

Noddings, N. (1995). Teaching themes of care. *Phi Delta Kappan, 76*(9), 675–679.

Nunner-Winkler, G. (1993). Two moralities? A critical discussion of an ethic of care and responsibility versus an ethic of rights and justice. In M. J. Larrabee (Ed.), *An ethic of care: Feminist and interdisciplinary perspectives.* New York: Routledge.

Ogbu, J. U. (1988). Class stratification, racial stratification, and schooling. In L. Weiss (Ed.), *Class, race, and gender in American education* (pp. 163–182). Albany: State University of New York Press.

Olsen, L. (1988). *Crossing the schoolhouse border: Immigrant students and the California public schools.* San Francisco: California Tomorrow.

Peshkin, A., & White, C. (1990). Four black American students: Coming of age in a multiethnic high school. *Teachers College Record, 92*(1), 21–37.

Quinn, D. (1992). *Ishmael: An adventure of the mind and spirit.* New York: Bantam.

Regan, H. B. (1990). Not for women only: School administration as a feminist activity. *Teachers College Record, 91*(4), 665–677.

Regan, H. B., & Brooks, G. H. (1995). *Out of women's experience: Creating relationship leadership.* Thousand Oaks, CA: Corwin Press.

Reiger, K. (1993). The gender dynamics of organizations: A historical account. In J. Blackmore & J. Kenway (Eds.), *Gender matters in educational administration and policy: A feminist introduction* (pp. 17–26). Bristol, PA: Falmer Press.

Rich, A. (1976). *Of woman born.* New York: Norton.

Rist, R. C. (1970). Student social class and teacher expectations: The self-fulfilling prophecy in ghetto education. *Harvard Educational Review, 40*(3), 411–451.

Ruether, R. R. (1975). *New woman, new earth: Sexist ideologies and human liberation.* New York: Seabury Press.

Rusch, E. A., & Marshall, C. (1995, April). *Gender filters at work in the administrative culture.* Paper presented at the annual meeting of the American Educational Research Association, San Francisco.

Sarason, S. B. (1982). *The culture of the school and the problem of change* (2nd ed.). Boston: Allyn & Bacon.

Sarton, M. (1978). *A reckoning.* New York: Norton.

Sarton, M. (1981). *The house by the sea.* New York: Norton.

Schaef, A. W. (1985). *Women's reality: An emerging female system in a white male society.* San Francisco: Harper & Row.

Schlechty, P. (1997, March 7). Informal breakfast discussion re learning, Indiana Spring Forum, Indianapolis.

Schorr, L. B. (1988). *Within our reach: Breaking the cycle of disadvantage.* New York: Doubleday.

Sedlak, M., Wheeler, C., Pullin, D., & Cusick, P. (1986). *Selling students short: Classroom bargains and academic reform in the American high school.* New York: Teachers College Press.

Sizer, T. R. (1985). *Horace's compromise: The dilemma of the American high school.* Boston: Houghton Mifflin.

Sizer, T. R. (1992). *Horace's school: Redesigning the American high school.* Boston: Houghton Mifflin.

Smircich, L. (1985, August). *Toward a woman centered organization theory.* Paper presented at the meeting of the Women in Management and Social Issues in Management Divisions of the Academy of Management, San Diego, CA.

Smircich, L., & Morgan, G. (1982). Leadership: The management of meaning. *Journal of Applied Behavioral Science, 18*(3), 257–273.

Stahl, L. (1993, May). *Sixty minutes* [Television broadcast]. New York: Central Broadcasting System.

Starratt, R. J. (1991). Building an ethical school: A theory for practice in educational leadership. *Educational Administration Quarterly, 27*(2), 185–202.

Taylor, C., Appiah, K. A., Habermas, J., Rockefeller, S. C., Walzer, M., & Wolf, S. (1994). *Multiculturalism: Examining the politics of recognition* (A. Gutman, Ed.). Princeton, NJ: Princeton University Press.

Taylor-Guthrie, D. (Ed.). (1994). *Conversations with Toni Morrison.* Jackson: University of Mississippi Press.

Tronto, J. C. (1987). Beyond gender difference to a theory of care. *Signs: Journal of Women in Culture and Society, 12*(4), 644–663.

Tronto, J. C. (1989). Women and caring: What can feminists learn about morality from caring? In A. M. Jaggar & S. R. Bordo (Eds.), *Gender/Body/Knowledge: Feminist reconstructions of being and knowing* (pp. 172–187). New Brunswick, NJ: Rutgers University Press.

Tronto, J. C. (1993). *Moral boundaries: A political argument for an ethic of care.* New York: Routledge.

Ungerson, C. (1983). Why do women care? In J. Finch & D. Groves (Eds.), *A labour of love: Women, work and caring* (pp. 31–50). London: Routledge & Kegan Paul.

Vanzant, I. (1993). *Acts of faith: Daily meditations for people of color.* New York: Simon & Schuster.

Weber, M. (1968). *Economy and society* (G. Roth & C. Wittich, Eds.). New York: Bedminster Press.

Weiler, K. (1988). *Women teaching for change: Gender, class & power.* South Hadley, MA: Bergin & Garvey.

Index

About the Author

Kathleen Sernak received her Ph.D. in Educational Policy and Social Analysis from Michigan State University. Her research focuses on the effect of technology and culture on one's identity, and on the sociology and history that influence women leaders whose cultural backgrounds are not Western European. She is interested in urban education and leadership in schools in low-income, culturally diverse areas. Currently, she is an Associate Professor in Educational Leadership at Rowan University.